**READ THE PASSAGE** Read slowly. Reread any section you do not understand.

I0890010

## Medical Practices in Ancient Egypt

### Learning About the Human Body

Today's medical examiners study the body parts of deceased people to learn about things that can be harmful and to help prevent illnesses. Ancient Egyptians also performed examinations on bodies to help understand causes of illness. Examinations helped ancient Egyptians learn about the human body. By comparing the hearts of people who were different ages, for example, Egyptians could determine what a young, healthy heart was supposed to look like.

### Keeping a Written Record

The Egyptians not only studied the human body, but they also kept detailed records of what they discovered. They wrote and drew their observations on papyrus, a form of paper. The papyrus records became the medical textbooks of that time. Their observations allowed Egyptian doctors to share their knowledge, including how to treat various diseases.

### Edwin Smith Papyrus

In 1862, an American named Edwin Smith purchased a medical papyrus in Luxor, Egypt. Smith was not a medical expert, but he knew a lot about old documents. He knew that what he had found was valuable. The papyrus turned out to be an ancient textbook on surgery. The papyrus was probably written around 1600 BC, but it was based on information from a thousand years before that. The papyrus presents the information as case studies, including an analysis of whether patients survived.

**STRATEGY PRACTICE** How did examinations help ancient Egyptians learn about the human body?

______________________________________________

______________________________________________

**SKILL PRACTICE** Read the item. Write your response.

1. What is this text mostly about?

______________________________________________

______________________________________________

2. What is the purpose of the headings?

______________________________________________

______________________________________________

3. What are doctors in 3020 most apt to learn from a medical textbook published in 2020?

______________________________________________

______________________________________________

**READ THE PASSAGE** Think about how the brothers behave.

## Ishmael and Isadore

Brothers Ishmael and Isadore were complete opposites. People who knew them both could hardly believe they were from the same planet, let alone the same family. The boys were not unkind toward one another, but their personalities were so different that it was difficult for them to reach a decision they both liked. Their mother frequently played the referee in their disagreements.

Ishmael, the older brother, was tall and athletic, and he loved sports. He played baseball, football, and basketball. Isadore, the younger brother, hated sports. He was quieter and less active than his brother. He preferred spending his time on the computer, making short videos and writing blog entries.

The brothers' taste in music was completely different, too. Ishmael loved classic rock. He listened to bands like the Beatles, the Who, and the Rolling Stones. Isadore didn't care much for those bands. He preferred spending his time streaming world music, especially music from Central Africa. Luckily for their parents, both boys enjoyed listening to music through headphones.

One other thing the brothers did agree on was that they wanted a pet. Mom had resisted getting one, but after both brothers had pleaded and begged, she finally agreed.

"We can get a pet, as long as you two take care of it," she said. "That means you do the feeding, you do the training, and if it needs to be walked, you do the walking."

"No problem, Mom," Ishmael and Isadore said together.

"Good, we all agree," Mom said. "Now, what kind of pet are we going to get?"

**STRATEGY PRACTICE** Was there any part of the passage that you didn't understand right away? How did you figure it out?

______________________________________________

______________________________________________

**SKILL PRACTICE** Read the item. Write your response.

1. What is the main idea of this text?

______________________________________________

______________________________________________

2. Predict what will happen next. Why do you think so?

______________________________________________

3. If the brothers choose a dog, who is most apt to take the dog running? Explain.

______________________________________________

______________________________________________

**READ THE PASSAGE** Underline or make notes about words you do not understand.

## Mayan Calendars

The Maya were an influential people living in what is now Guatemala, Belize, Honduras, El Salvador, and parts of southern Mexico. The ancient Maya developed sophisticated systems of agriculture, architecture, science, mathematics, and writing. One of the most important Mayan developments was the creation of calendars.

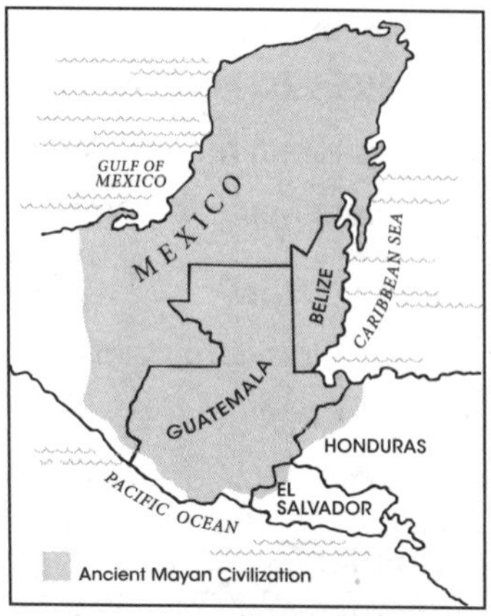


The ancient Maya had three calendars. Two of them were the Tzolkin (ZOL-keen) calendar, which was tied to religious beliefs, and the Haab (hayb) calendar, which was based on the length of a year.

Understanding astronomy helped the Maya accurately measure days, months, and years. A year had 365 days by Mayan calculations, as it does in our own calendar. The Mayan year, though, was made up of 18 months, and each month had 20 days. An extra 5 days were added to complete the calendar year. These days rounded out the calendar nicely, but the Maya thought they were unlucky.

One of the most unusual Mayan calendars was actually a pyramid. Around AD 1050, the Maya built the Pyramid of Kukulkan (KO-KUL-kan) at Chichén Itzá (CHEE-chen EET-sah). The pyramid had a stairway on each of its four sides. Each stairway had 91 steps. Counting the platform at the top, there were 365 steps, the same number of days in the calendar year.

**STRATEGY PRACTICE** List one or two words you found confusing and describe how you figured out their meanings.

______________________________

**SKILL PRACTICE** Read the item. Write your response.

1. What is the second paragraph mostly about?

______________________________

______________________________

2. Why did the author include a map?

______________________________

______________________________

3. Cite the part of the sentence that supports the idea that the Pyramid of Kukulkan was a calendar.

______________________________

______________________________

**READ THE PASSAGE** Read slowly and think about the main idea of each section.

## Ancient and Modern Chinese Characters

### In the Beginning

When people write in English, they use letters of the alphabet. People who write in Chinese, however, use characters that stand for words or ideas. Historians believe Chinese writing began as early as 1500 BC. The earliest forms were called "oracle bones." These were animal bones marked with pictures and symbols. In addition to writing on bones, the Chinese also made marks on turtle shells. By 1400 BC, the Chinese writing system had become more complex. It had more than 2,500 characters. Around 200 BC, Chinese characters became standardized. This means that everyone used the same characters.

### Then and Now

Many modern Chinese characters are similar to those from 2,000 years ago. For example, the character that means *man* in the Lishu system from 200 BC is similar to the character that means *man* from the Jiantizi, or modern simplified system, of the twentieth century.

### A Simpler System

People have made efforts to change Chinese characters over the centuries. The most important changes happened in the twentieth century. The Chinese government simplified many characters so that more people could learn to read. Both this simpler system and traditional characters are now used in different areas. Even with these changes, Chinese writing from 2,200 years ago is still understood today.

**STRATEGY PRACTICE** Did you understand the main points the writer makes? Why or why not?

______________________________________________

**SKILL PRACTICE** Read the item. Write your response.

1. How do the headings in this text help the reader?

______________________________________________

______________________________________________

2. What is the main idea of the text?

______________________________________________

______________________________________________

3. Which fact from the text supports the idea that ancient and modern Chinese characters are similar?

______________________________________________

______________________________________________

**READ THE PASSAGE** Read slowly and pause after each paragraph.

## Colossus of Rhodes

The Colossus of Rhodes, a giant bronze statue, was one of the Seven Wonders of the Ancient World. Other ancient civilizations also built large statues, but the Colossus of Rhodes was one of the tallest. At more than 105 feet (32 meters) tall, it was twice as big as most of the other colossi (kuh-LOSS-eye), or giant statues, of ancient times. The Statue of Liberty, its modern counterpart, is only slightly taller.

The Colossus of Rhodes was designed and built by the sculptor Chares (CHAR-eez) of Lindos. It showed the sun god Helios. The people of the Greek island of Rhodes had it built to celebrate the defeat of Demetrius I in 305 BC. Chares and the artists in his workshop began building the statue in 292 BC. The Colossus was completed twelve years later. It welcomed friends and warned foes as they approached the island's harbor.

Unfortunately, the statue stood for only 56 years. In 224 BC, a powerful earthquake hit Rhodes. The quake damaged the Colossus, and it fell to the ground in giant pieces. The statue's parts lay on the ground for hundreds of years, and travelers came from all over to see these impressive ruins.

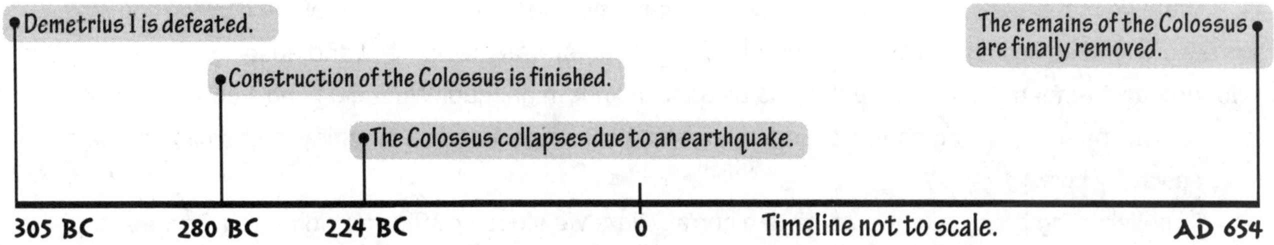


**STRATEGY PRACTICE** List two important facts about the Colossus of Rhodes.

______________________________________________

______________________________________________

**SKILL PRACTICE** Read the item. Write your response.

1. In what year was the Colossus of Rhodes completed? How do you know?

______________________________________________

______________________________________________

2. Why was the Colossus of Rhodes one of the Seven Wonders of the Ancient World?

______________________________________________

______________________________________________

3. What information does the timeline give you that the text does not?

______________________________________________

**READ THE MEMOIR** Think about how the writer probably feels.

## Up to the Mountaintop

I like challenges, but this one was almost too difficult. I had begged Mom to take me on a completely new adventure for my sixteenth birthday. Now, here we were, just Mom and me with our guide, Milo, standing on the shore of Lake Arenal in Costa Rica. Towering above the lake was Volcán Arenal, one of the active volcanoes in the region. I watched as the volcano spit out lava and coughed up big boulders. Luckily, we were headed in the other direction.

Milo greeted us in Spanish and helped us mount our horses. Getting on my horse was difficult, but controlling it was a little easier. We started on our tour. The guidebook said we'd cross three rivers. As we splashed through a stream, I asked, "Was that the first river?"

"I don't think so, Katie," Mom said wryly.

Soon enough, we came to the first river. There was no mistaking it. I felt sick to my stomach when I saw that the far shore was half a football field away! The 4-foot-deep (1.2 m) river flowed over boulders. So much for dry shoes—or jeans.

After two more rivers, the trail got even steeper and muddier. With each step of the horses' hooves, there were loud squishing and sucking sounds. The rainforest was magnificent and absolutely beautiful. But I wondered whether my horse could keep its balance in knee-high mud. What did I know about horses? I imagined my mare stumbling on rocks hidden beneath the sludge—and us crashing over a cliff and being swept away by lava.

Three terrifying hours later, we came to a corral. Were we stopping? To one side was a gorgeous view of the lake and volcano, and to the other, a brightly painted restaurant. "Okay," I laughed nervously. "That was terrifying, but I'm so glad we did it!"

**STRATEGY PRACTICE** Describe a personal experience that is similar to Katie's experience.

______________________________

______________________________

**SKILL PRACTICE** Read the item. Write your response.

1. Describe the setting of this memoir.

______________________________

______________________________

2. Draw an inference about Katie's experience riding horses.

______________________________

3. Name two adjectives that describe Katie. Explain your choices.

______________________________

**READ THE PASSAGE** Think about what Jeff Biggs does and how he feels about his job.

## Dirty Job? Oh Yeah!

"You couldn't pay me to do that job!" Have you ever said that? Some occupations are so gross that most people would never be willing to do them.

Jeff Biggs has a job like that, but he likes it. He's the kind of guy who, as a kid, loved to slosh around in mud after a rainstorm; the kind of kid who loved squeezing oatmeal through his fingers.

Biggs's dirty job is being a sewer inspector. "Believe me," says Biggs, "gross doesn't come close to describing it. I creep, sometimes swim, through sewage all day." City sewers carry household wastewater and storm-drain runoff to water treatment plants. In addition to the unpleasant smells, sewer tunnels are home to creatures such as cockroaches and rats. And these creatures aren't shy.

What is it like to do a really disgusting job day after day? "Someone has to do it," says Biggs. "I seriously can't imagine sitting in an office all day, and I earn a good salary. At the end of my workday, I've accomplished something, and I've helped to keep our city's water clean and drinkable."

And after work? "I don't walk into the house right away," explains Biggs. "We installed the washing machine in the garage and put a shower stall in there, too. I toss my clothes into the washer, take a shower, and dress in clean clothes. Then I greet my family. Of course, sometimes, the clothes go into the trash, not the washer."

**STRATEGY PRACTICE** What would happen if no one performed jobs like the one Jeff Biggs has?

______________________________________________

______________________________________________

**SKILL PRACTICE** Read the item. Write your response.

1. Name two adjectives that describe Jeff Biggs's working environment. Explain your choices.

______________________________________________

______________________________________________

2. What did the author mean by the statement "And these creatures aren't shy"?

______________________________________________

______________________________________________

3. Describe Jeff Biggs's attitude toward his occupation.

______________________________________________

______________________________________________

**READ THE LETTER** Think about how people today and from long ago have dealt with natural disasters.

# A Letter from Antioch

Antioch, Syria
Saturday, May 23, AD 526

Dear Father,

I write to tell you the shocking news that has happened since your departure last month. On Wednesday, Antioch suffered a terrible earthquake. Mother and I are safe, and our house is damaged but still standing. However, over 220,000 people in the city have died, and officials expect even higher numbers as the survivors search the rubble for their loved ones. Hundreds are fleeing the city, carrying their few undamaged belongings on their backs.

Many of the familiar churches, markets, theaters, and monuments have been destroyed. Some buildings that withstood the initial quake collapsed during aftershocks. One of the saddest losses was the Great Church. Although it survived the aftershocks, it caught fire yesterday and burned.

Looters are going into collapsed buildings and stealing valuables. Thieves have attacked some people who are fleeing the city. But all hope is not lost. Just this morning, brave people rescued a young woman and her child from the ruins of a house. As I write, volunteers are retrieving many of our pieces of fine mosaic art. They are loading them into boats to transport them to other locations. And messengers arrived from Emperor Justin this morning. He has pledged to help us rebuild.

I wish you a safe journey and urge caution on your return.

Your son,
Simeon

**STRATEGY PRACTICE** Do you think people in the past reacted any differently to disasters from the way people do today? Explain.

______________________________

______________________________

**SKILL PRACTICE** Read the item. Write your response.

1. How does Simeon feel about Antioch?

______________________________

______________________________

2. Why are people fleeing the city?

______________________________

3. What two opposing realities are revealed in the third paragraph?

______________________________

______________________________

**READ THE FOLK TALE** Look for phrases or ideas that remind you of other folk tales.

## The Elephant and the Hummingbird

Long, long ago—in the days when people could talk to animals and learn their stories—an elephant walked slowly beside the Yellow River. This was before animals were tamed, even before the first Chinese emperors ruled. That's how long ago it was.

The elephant was enjoying a peaceful stroll. Thick grasses and beautiful lotus flowers bloomed, and the water in the Yellow River made a pleasant swishing sound as it flowed past the elephant.

Noticing what appeared to be a hummingbird, the elephant stopped. Although they don't exist in China today, the elephant had seen hummingbirds before. He'd watched them hover above lotus flowers, their wings beating so quickly that they appeared only as a blur. The elephant sometimes wished he could move as quickly as a hummingbird. This one, however, was lying upside down, her wings motionless and her legs pointing toward the sky. Occasionally, the little bird would sigh heavily or grunt, as if working extra hard.

"What are you doing?" asked the elephant. He slowly walked around the hummingbird, trying to understand the odd behavior. "You look ridiculous, you know."

"I am holding up the sky," replied the hummingbird calmly. "I overheard that it might fall today."

The elephant raised his trunk and made a sound that today might pass as a deep laugh. "You're holding up the sky? Why, just look at it. The sky is bigger than I am, and I doubt you could hold me up. Even if the sky were going to fall, your tiny legs could not possibly do the job."

"Ah," said the hummingbird, "but these are the only legs I have. I might not be able to do it by myself, but I am doing what I can."

**STRATEGY PRACTICE** Describe a story, movie, or experience that this folk tale reminds you of.

______________________________________________

______________________________________________

**SKILL PRACTICE** Read the item. Write your response.

1. When and where does this folk tale take place?

______________________________________________

______________________________________________

2. What does the elephant think of the hummingbird's explanation? How do you know?

______________________________________________

______________________________________________

3. What is the lesson, or moral, of the text?

______________________________________________

______________________________________________

**READ THE PASSAGE** Look for descriptions of things or practices that have changed since 1899.

## Newsies Strike New York

Today, people can buy a newspaper online, from a machine, or at a newsstand. But back in the 1800s, newsboys, or "newsies," were the principal sellers of newspapers. Newsies sold their newspapers, or "papes," on New York's streets. Newsies bought their newspapers from the companies that printed them. The newsboys then made their money by selling the newspapers to customers.

For two weeks in 1899, however, the newsies went on strike, refusing to sell papers. Boys from 5 to 15 years old united to make two newspaper companies reduce the price that they charged newsies for the newspapers. Striking newsboys held rallies, gave speeches, and chose leaders. One rally drew more than 7,000 striking newsies. Newsboys who continued to sell papers were harassed by the strikers. Some strikers threw the newspapers away, and others threatened to hurt the newsboys who wouldn't stop selling newspapers.

What started the strike? During the Spanish-American War, people were eager to read the news, so the *Journal* and *Evening World* raised the price that they charged for their newspapers. Newsies had to pay ten cents more for the papers. A dime made a difference to the kids who earned less than a dollar each day. Most newsies lived on the streets. Others used their earnings to help their struggling families. When the war ended, newsies expected newspaper companies to reduce their prices, but that did not happen.

Although the cost of papers to newsies never dropped, the strike was considered a success. The two offending newspaper companies agreed to buy back all unsold papers, and eventually this strike helped bring about child labor laws in the United States.

**STRATEGY PRACTICE** What does the newsies' strike of 1899 remind you of today?

______________________________________________

______________________________________________

**SKILL PRACTICE** Read the item. Write your response.

1. What lesson can you learn from the newsies' strike?

______________________________________________

______________________________________________

2. How do you think the strike helped to bring about labor laws?

______________________________________________

______________________________________________

3. Based on the information in the passage, name three common characteristics among newsboys.

______________________________________________

______________________________________________

**READ THE PASSAGE** Read slowly and pay attention to details that help you make a mental picture.

## Forests of Clouds and Mist

You've probably heard of rainforests, but do you know what a cloud forest is? Cloud forests are evergreen forests that are often covered in clouds or mist and are located on mountains. Cool temperatures on mountain slopes create clouds that cover the trees. There are cloud forests on most continents. Central and South America have them, as do Asia and Africa. You can also find cloud forests in Hawaii and on Caribbean islands.

Cloud forests have different names, depending on where they are found. Cloud forests are also known as fog forests or mossy forests. In Peru and Bolivia, cloud forests are part of a larger ecosystem called *yungas,* which means "warm lands."

Many scientists consider cloud forests to be a special type of rainforest. Cloud forests are not as warm as tropical rainforests because they are found at higher elevations that have colder air. But cloud forests and tropical rainforests both have many different plants and animals living within their ecosystems.

Like tropical rainforests, cloud forest trees drip with moisture, but it does not often rain in a cloud forest. Instead, the fog collects as dew on leaves, vines, and branches. This dew provides the water that the plants need. Green moss, ferns, and exotic, colorful orchid flowers hang down from the canopy. Other plants and bushes crowd between the trees, and hundreds of insects crawl and fly amid the vegetation. Cloud forests are as diverse and interesting as rainforests or temperate forests.

Cloud forests have animals that aren't found anywhere else, such as mountain gorillas and a strange woolly mammal called the mountain tapir. The colorful quetzal bird is also found there, and golden toads hop among the bushes. Recently, scientists discovered a new cloud forest animal, a black and brown rodent that looks like a cross between a squirrel and a rat. Cloud forests probably contain hundreds of other rare and fascinating plants and animals that people have never seen before.

**STRATEGY PRACTICE** Underline words or phrases in the passage that you were able to visualize.

**SKILL PRACTICE** Read the item. Write your response.

1. Why was it essential to visualize as you read this text?

______________________________

______________________________

2. How do cloud forests differ from tropical rainforests?

______________________________

______________________________

3. Picture yourself walking in a cloud forest. Briefly describe the experience.

______________________________

______________________________

**READ THE PASSAGE** Look for words that help you form a mental picture.

## Kids Take to the Airwaves

On the first Sunday in March each year, kids get to take over the world's airwaves. The United Nations Children's Fund (UNICEF) has designated that day as the International Children's Day of Broadcasting, or ICDB. Television and radio stations around the world invite young people to be part of their programming. Thousands of broadcasters and kids participate, and the programs focus on children's interests and issues. Kids are also involved in the broadcast process, learning how radio and television programs are made. ICDB gives children a voice that can be heard around the world.

On ICDB in 2009, young people all over the globe reported on issues that affected them. Nearly 100 children from India recorded stories about a flood in their area. Children in China drew pictures with messages for their parents. In Senegal, young people spoke out against violence by giving reports, conducting interviews, writing poems, and singing songs. German children talked with young people in Serbia and shared drawings and photographs. Australian kids voiced their opinions to children in Cambodia, Fiji, and Tonga. Kids produced videos on a variety of different topics, from air pollution to loneliness. Across the world, young people expressed their feelings and sent messages about what mattered most to them.

After ICDB is over, UNICEF holds a contest for the best radio or television program. People who make the programs that air during ICDB can submit their programs. The winners attend a special celebration. The 2009 radio winner was a station in Brazil that broadcasted a show for 24 hours about children from poor communities. The show used interviews, diaries, and music to promote peace. The winner for the television program was a station in Kenya. The show, which was hosted by two Kenyan youths, talked about the challenges that Kenyan children face and highlighted positive stories about young people in their communities.

**STRATEGY PRACTICE** Write three nouns (people, places, or things) that were easy for you to picture.

______________________________________________

**SKILL PRACTICE** Read the item. Write your response.

1. What is the purpose of International Children's Day of Broadcasting?

______________________________________________

______________________________________________

2. Describe the mental image that was easiest for you to form as you read the second paragraph.

______________________________________________

______________________________________________

3. What is the first paragraph mainly about?

______________________________________________

______________________________________________

**READ THE PASSAGE** As you read, adjust your mental image when you come across new details.

## Not Quite the Same

When most people want to see what they look like, they look in a mirror. I don't need a mirror to see myself, though. I can just look at my identical twin sister, Sarita.

Sarita and I have always worn our hair the same way—long and straight, with bangs. We have the same dark eyes and big smile, and we both have one crooked tooth on the right. We both love the color green, hate eating fish, and think mayonnaise is disgusting. We play the violin, and every year we compete with each other for the position of first violin in the school orchestra.

In some ways, however, we're totally different. Sarita always wears funky hats, which I think is really weird. She thinks it's strange that I like jazz music. Some people say that our biggest difference is that Sarita is in a wheelchair. She was in a car accident when she was very young, and her spine was badly injured. To me, however, the real difference between us is that Sarita has courage and determination. She has never let being in a wheelchair slow her down, and she's almost never angry or unhappy about what happened to her. So when I look in the mirror, I see myself—Celia—but I also see Sarita, a better version of me. She's the me I *try* to be.

**STRATEGY PRACTICE** Sketch how you visualized the two girls.

**SKILL PRACTICE** Read the item. Write your response.

1. Name three ways in which the girls are similar.

______________________________________________

______________________________________________

2. Name three ways in which the girls are different.

______________________________________________

______________________________________________

3. Why does Celia admire Sarita?

______________________________________________

______________________________________________

**READ THE PASSAGE** Look for strong verbs and clear nouns and adjectives.

## A Plane in the Hudson River

Some airplanes are made specifically to land on water, but US Airways Flight 1549 was not one of those planes. The plane took off from LaGuardia Airport on January 15, 2009, with 155 people on board. Just three minutes later, the pilot, Captain Chesley Sullenberger, radioed that the plane was in trouble. It had hit some large geese. The left engine had exploded in fire, smoke, and metal.

Captain Sullenberger quickly realized that the plane could not make it back to the airport. The aircraft was rapidly losing power and would soon be too slow to stay in the air. Sullenberger turned the plane toward the Hudson River, which flows between New York and New Jersey.

"Brace for impact!" Captain Sullenberger announced over the intercom. Many passengers were tense and scared, but the flight crew did their best to keep everyone calm. Most passengers lowered their heads and got ready for a rough crash landing.

After several tension-filled minutes, Captain Sullenberger landed the plane perfectly on the surface of the Hudson River. People watching from ferries that were traveling between New York and New Jersey were shocked at the sight. The plane's passengers climbed onto the wings as the plane began to fill with water and sink. Boats from both sides of the river rushed to aid the stranded passengers. The waters were icy cold, and the smell of gasoline filled the air. As passengers scrambled from the plane to the waiting boats, rescuers handed them blankets, coats, and life jackets to stay warm.

All 155 people were brought to safety, and Captain Sullenberger was celebrated as a hero. It was the first time a major aircraft had ever crash-landed in water with no deaths.

**STRATEGY PRACTICE** Underline the verbs and draw a box around the adjectives that helped you visualize the scene as you read.

**SKILL PRACTICE** Read the item. Write your response.

1. What caused the plane's left engine to stop functioning?

______________________________

______________________________

2. How did this emergency water landing differ from all others?

______________________________

______________________________

3. Why is it a good thing that this event happened in a busy city?

______________________________

______________________________

**READ THE PASSAGE** Make a mental image of the events described in the passage.

## The World's Biggest Wave

A tsunami is a giant ocean wave. It is usually created by an earthquake on the seafloor and can travel hundreds or even thousands of miles across the ocean. The biggest local tsunami ever to hit land happened on July 9, 1958, when an earthquake shook the undersea fault near Lituya Bay, Alaska. Lituya Bay is part of Alaska's Glacier Bay National Park. The magnitude 8.0 earthquake shook 40 million cubic yards (31 million cubic meters) of dirt, rocks, and ice from a mountain at the head of the bay. The landslide fell 3,000 feet (914 meters) and hit the water with tremendous force, which created the enormous tsunami wave. The wave was more than 1,640 feet (500 meters) high and crashed over five square miles (13 square kilometers) of land, uprooting millions of trees.

There were no towns in the area, so unlike the deadly tsunami of 2004, in which more than 200,000 people in Indonesia and elsewhere were killed, the 1958 tsunami killed only two people. They were on a fishing boat anchored in the bay when the wave swamped them. Another boat, the Badger, was carrying William Swanson and his wife. The boat rode the wave inland before it began to sink. The Swansons were able to leap to a small skiff and were rescued a few hours later. A third boat, the Edrie, with Howard Ulrich and his seven-year-old son aboard, rode the wave over land and then back out to the bay. The Ulriches, amazingly, were unharmed.

For many years, scientists debated about what really caused the tsunami in Lituya Bay. Some scientists claimed the amount of debris that fell into the bay was not enough to cause such a massive wave. They thought that the earthquake itself triggered the wave. However, as our understanding of geology, earthquakes, and tsunamis has improved, most scientists now accept the rockslide as the true cause for the wave. No one disputes, however, that the wave was the largest ever recorded and will likely remain so for years to come.

**STRATEGY PRACTICE** Describe to a partner the parts of the passage you thought were the most important to visualize in order to understand the main idea of the passage.

**SKILL PRACTICE** Read the item. Write your response.

1. The average skyscraper is 350 feet (107 m) tall. How does knowing this fact help you envision the wave discussed in the text?

___

2. How did the 1958 and 2004 tsunamis differ?

___

___

3. Was the cause of the 1958 tsunami the typical cause? Explain.

___

___

 

**READ THE PASSAGE** Look for important events in the life of Sarah Edmonds.

## Soldier in Disguise

In April 1863, a Civil War soldier known as Franklin Thompson deserted from the Union Army. Thompson was sick with malaria but was afraid to go to an army hospital. What was Thompson so afraid of? His real name was Sarah Edmonds—and "he" was one of hundreds of women who pretended to be men so that they could fight in the Civil War.

Edmonds was born in Canada in 1841 and came to the United States in 1858. She disguised herself as Franklin Thompson and worked as a book salesman. In May 1861, one month after the Civil War began, she enlisted in the Second Michigan Infantry.

For two years, Edmonds served in the army as Private Thompson. The Second Michigan Infantry fought in some important and violent battles, including First Bull Run in July 1861, Antietam in September 1862, and Fredericksburg in December 1862. Edmonds kept her gender a secret by sleeping in her own tent and sneaking off to bathe privately.

Upon leaving the army, Edmonds resumed her real identity. She eventually revealed her service as Thompson in order to get a pension as a Civil War soldier. In 1886, the War Department recognized her as a female soldier who had served faithfully as a private during the war. She received the $12-a-month pension and was cleared of the desertion charge. When she died in 1898, Edmonds was buried with military honors.

**STRATEGY PRACTICE** How does adding dates to the passage help organize it?

______________________________

______________________________

**SKILL PRACTICE** Read the item. Write your response.

1. Why did Franklin Thompson desert from the Union Army?

______________________________

______________________________

2. What caused Edmonds to reveal the truth about her identity?

______________________________

______________________________

3. Why did Edmonds receive military honors at her funeral?

______________________________

______________________________

**READ THE PASSAGE** Think about how the author introduces each paragraph.

## Facts About Water

**Drink of the Dinos** Water is as old as Earth itself. Look at a glass of water. It might contain the same drops that a dinosaur drank millions of years ago. It could have made up the first rainbow you ever saw or a river that your ancestors fished in. It could have snowed on the Alps or been part of a worm or a carrot. It could have carved a canyon or been pumped up from a well. Water constantly recycles itself as rain, vapor, ice, fog, or snow. Over a period of 100 years, a drop of water will spend 98 years as ocean, 20 months as ice, 2 weeks in a river or lake, and less than a week in the air. It will spend the rest of its time in living things.

**Liquid for Life** Earth is the only planet known to have liquid water on its surface. That is why life can exist here. The human body is about two-thirds water. You might guess that our blood is mostly water, but there is even water in our bones. An elephant is 70% water, and a tomato is 95% water. Water carries oxygen and breaks down food. It also carries waste out of our bodies. Plants use water to make food and move nutrients around. Over half of the world's plants and animals use fresh or ocean water as a home.

**Power of Water** Water shapes land more than anything else. Waves eat away coastlines. Glaciers cut valleys. Rivers break down mountains and carve canyons. Water's movement also provides power we can use. It flows through turbines, machines with blades. Water spins the blades, making electricity.

**STRATEGY PRACTICE** How does the author organize information about water?

______________________________________________

______________________________________________

**SKILL PRACTICE** Read the item. Write your response.

1. What would be a better title for this passage?

______________________________________________

______________________________________________

2. Why do you think water is sometimes called "liquid gold"?

______________________________________________

______________________________________________

3. Water can be liquid, solid, or gas. Which form do you think it is in the least often? Explain your thinking.

______________________________________________

______________________________________________

**READ THE PASSAGE** Look for the causes and effects of the python problem in Florida.

## Florida's Python Problem

Sometimes pets are more than we can handle, like when a small puppy grows up to be a huge dog. People can usually find a new home for a big dog, but a giant pet snake is not so easy to give away. As a result, some people in Florida have released their pet pythons into the wilderness of the Florida Everglades. Problem solved? Only for the pet owners.

The snakes that are the biggest problem are Burmese pythons. These snakes are not native to the Everglades. Pet dealers originally brought them to the United States from Southeast Asia. Because Burmese pythons are not native, they disrupt the natural order of the Everglades' ecosystem.

The snakes' size and strength are also a problem. Burmese pythons can grow to be 20 feet (6 m) long. There are reports of terrifying battles between pythons and alligators in the Everglades. Even more worrisome is the impact on creatures that are no match for the monster snakes. For example, biologists have discovered endangered birds, bobcats, and wood rats in pythons' stomachs.

Another effect of python dumping is the spread of these snakes beyond the Everglades. Pythons swim well and can move more than a mile a day on land. In addition, one snake can produce nearly 100 eggs. Their wide range of movement and high rate of birth means that the snakes can quickly overrun a habitat.

As a result of this scary scenario, Florida park rangers, wildlife officials, and others are on "python patrol." They capture and kill Burmese pythons to try to keep the numbers under control. There is also a greater effort to teach people about the responsibilities of keeping a python.

**STRATEGY PRACTICE** Underline the words in the passage that signal cause and effect.

**SKILL PRACTICE** Read the item. Write your response.

1. How did Burmese pythons end up in the Florida Everglades?

2. What problems are pythons causing in Florida?

3. Why are pythons spreading beyond the Everglades?

 

**READ THE PASSAGE** Think about the order in which the events in the passage occurred.

## Growing Good Examples at the White House

In 2009, people praised First Lady Michelle Obama for planting a vegetable garden soon after moving into the White House. The hope was that growing vegetables on the White House lawn would encourage Americans to eat more healthfully and motivate other families to grow fresh produce, too. It might seem like a new idea to plant a presidential garden to influence national behavior. However, earlier presidents and first ladies also used the White House grounds to set a good example.

In 1943, during World War II, First Lady Eleanor Roosevelt planted a "victory garden" at the White House. The goal was to get Americans to grow small gardens to feed themselves. That way, more food was available to send to American soldiers fighting overseas. Mrs. Roosevelt was widely admired, and her garden inspired many families to plant more food for themselves.

Twenty-five years earlier, during World War I, President Woodrow Wilson used the White House lawn to send a message to Americans. Wilson brought in a flock of sheep to cut the grass. It was a novel way to show how to use "natural resources" during wartime.

There was a time when a vegetable garden at the White House was simply practical. President John Adams planted the first garden in 1800. Adams didn't need to set an example, since most of the nation were already farmers. He just wanted food for his family and guests to eat!

**STRATEGY PRACTICE** Why do you think the author chose this way of organizing the passage?

______________________________

______________________________

**SKILL PRACTICE** Read the item. Write your response.

1. What evidence does the text offer that the former first family's influence on the nation's behavior was *not* a new idea?

______________________________

______________________________

2. What resource was conserved by using sheep to keep the White House lawn trimmed?

______________________________

______________________________

3. What was the purpose of the earliest White House garden?

______________________________

______________________________

**READ THE PASSAGE** Think about how the author introduces each character and tells the events in the story.

## Three Parts for Three Characters

Denzel could hear the sounds of the song "Follow the Yellow Brick Road" as he walked closer to the auditorium. He was relieved that the auditions weren't over. He really wanted to try out for the sixth-grade production of *The Wizard of Oz*. Waiting in the hall were his two best friends, Colin and Felipe. Colin was walking on his hands in a wide circle. Then he did a back flip, a cartwheel, and a backward leap into a handstand. Felipe was doing his favorite herky-jerky robot dance.

Just as Denzel reached the boys, there was a sudden boom outside. "What was that?" Denzel shouted. He had a voice that could be loud and strong one moment and drop to a whisper the next instant.

"It's thunder," Colin laughed. "You should audition for the role of the character who needs courage!"

"Come on!" Felipe urged with a stiff turn and bow to end his dance. "We'll miss our turns!"

The trio hurried inside the auditorium. A girl named Rachel, with hair teased like a lion's mane, was beginning her audition. The boys watched her. She pranced around the stage like a lion, but she spoke very quietly, and it was hard to hear her. When she finished, Felipe auditioned by dancing like a robot. Colin went next, showing his acrobatic skills. Denzel went last.

When the auditions ended, each boy had the perfect part for his talents. Colin was the Scarecrow, who is supposed to flop, slip, and slide all over the stage. Felipe's robot moves were just like the Tin Man in his rusty metal suit. And Denzel's booming roar and soft whisper made him the best Cowardly Lion the play could have.

**STRATEGY PRACTICE** If the author began the story by telling you what part each boy received, how would it change your reaction to the story?

______________________________________________

______________________________________________

**SKILL PRACTICE** Read the item. Write your response.

1. What is the purpose of these auditions?

______________________________________________

______________________________________________

2. How did Rachel probably feel at the end of the story?

______________________________________________

______________________________________________

3. How do Colin's words foreshadow the story's ending?

______________________________________________

______________________________________________

**READ THE WEB PAGE** Look at each section carefully to understand what the web page is about.

# Welcome to the SPORT POD

**Are you looking for up-to-date scores?**

**Do you want more information about your favorite players?**

**Would you like to connect with passionate fans just like you?**

**You've come to the right place! The SPORT POD is the only sports website you'll ever need.**

The **SPORT POD** has more features than any other site out there, including:

- **live scores from baseball, football, basketball, soccer, hockey, tennis, lacrosse, cricket, bowling, volleyball, table tennis, and other sports around the world**
- **pre-game predictions and post-game analysis by experts**
- **strategy hints and scoring tips that can help you improve your game**
- **message boards where you can exchange information with players and other fans**
- **personal home pages that allow you to track your favorite teams and players**

**You are just ONE CLICK away! Best of all, you can use the SPORT POD completely FREE.***

**YES, sign me up right away!**

**No thanks, not right now.**

*New users get free access for the first 90 days of their membership.

**STRATEGY PRACTICE** Describe what the SPORT POD is and what this web page is mostly about.

______________________________________________

______________________________________________

**SKILL PRACTICE** Read the item. Write your response.

1. What is the purpose of the phrases next to the handprints?

______________________________________________

______________________________________________

2. Why is the "yes" button highlighted?

______________________________________________

______________________________________________

3. Look at the asterisk at the bottom right corner of the web page. What does it explain?

______________________________________________

______________________________________________

**READ THE PASSAGE** Read the passage and study the line graph.

# Internet Boom

Today the Internet is widely used in homes, schools, and businesses around the world. However, that hasn't always been the case. The Internet was first developed in the 1960s and 1970s by U.S. government scientists as a way of sharing information. The earliest version of the Internet was called ARPAnet, for Advanced Research Projects Agency network. In 1969, only four computers were connected to the ARPAnet. Just 20 years later, though, as computers became more commonly developed, over 80,000 computers were connected.

Use of the Internet has continued to grow dramatically. Experts estimate that about 1% of the world's population used the Internet in 1996. By 2016, that percentage grew to over 43%.

How do researchers count more than 1 billion users? Programs called web crawlers browse the Internet to monitor how many pages and users are out there. Web crawlers work automatically, collecting data once they are started. These programs are sometimes called "spiders" because they "crawl" around the web.

As the Internet continues to grow, an increasing number of spiders scurry invisibly, collecting and sending information 24 hours a day.

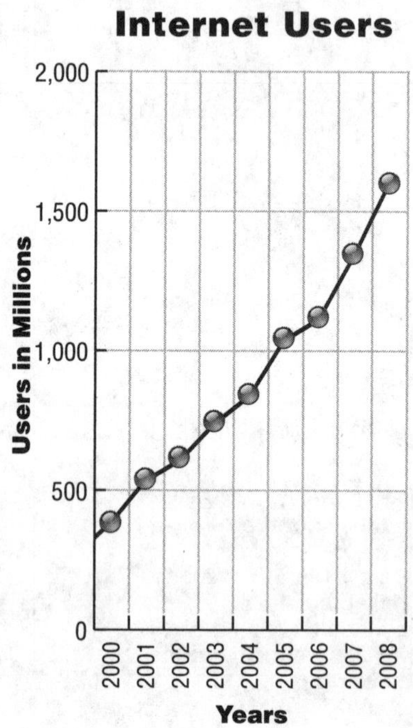


**STRATEGY PRACTICE** What trend about Internet users does the graph show?

______________________________________________

**SKILL PRACTICE** Read the item. Write your response.

1. What is the purpose of the graph?

______________________________________________

______________________________________________

2. What information does the text give in the third paragraph that cannot be determined from the graph?

______________________________________________

______________________________________________

3. Why does the text mention billions of users in the third paragraph when the graph shows millions?

______________________________________________

______________________________________________

**READ THE INDEX** Read the index and the passage from a book about planets and space.

## Index to
*The Planets and Beyond*

Each entry in this index is followed by the page numbers where the entry is discussed. Page numbers in **boldface** type indicate pages on which entries are defined. Page numbers in *italic* type indicate pages on which illustrations or photographs appear. The abbreviation "**Pr**" indicates a page on which the entry is used in a project.

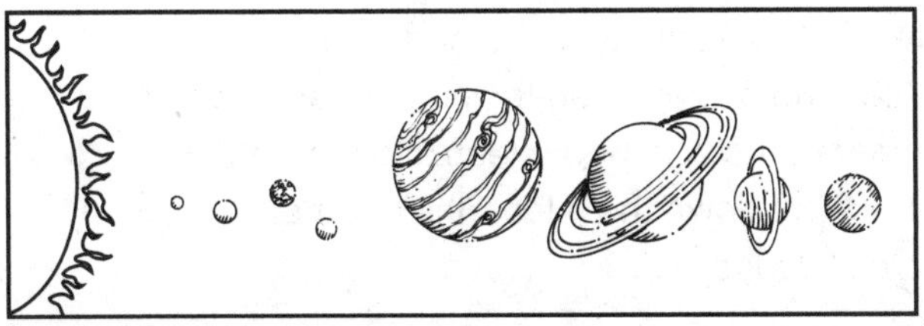



**STRATEGY PRACTICE** Describe the type of person who would need this book.

______________________________________________

______________________________________________

**SKILL PRACTICE** Read the item. Write your response.

1. On which page would you find the definition of a comet? How can you tell?

______________________________________________

______________________________________________

2. On which page(s) would you look to see an image of an aurora? How do you know?

______________________________________________

______________________________________________

3. What is the purpose of the first indented entry beneath "Atmosphere"?

______________________________________________

______________________________________________

## Determine Important Information

**READ THE COLUMN** Read the question carefully before you read the response.

### ASK Dr. Science

**Dear Dr. Science:**
I couldn't sleep at all last night. My sister says it was because I ate a bowl of really spicy chili right before bedtime, but I think that's ridiculous. Can spicy foods at bedtime really affect your sleep?
—*Sleepless in Secaucus*

**Dear Sleepless:**
I know where you're coming from, as I often munch on jalapeño peppers before lights out. What does science say?

Researchers in Australia did an experiment to find out the effects of spicy foods on sleep patterns. They gave a group of people tasty late-night meals. Some nights, they got spicy meals with ingredients such as hot sauce and mustard. Other nights, their meals were mild.

It turns out that your sister is on to something. When participants ate spicy foods, their sleep patterns were changed. They took longer to fall asleep and they slept less overall, too.

Researchers aren't sure exactly how spicy foods change sleep patterns, but they have some theories. It could be due to simple stomach upset or indigestion. But they also suspect that body temperature plays a role. Spicy foods include a chemical that can raise the body's temperature. Other studies have connected increased body temperatures with poor sleep. So before you go to bed, put down the jalapeños and hot sauce!
—*Dr. Science*

**STRATEGY PRACTICE** **If you were writing a research report about sleep studies, what part of this column would you refer to?**

______________________________________________

**SKILL PRACTICE** Read the item. Write your response.

1. **Where might you find this type of text?**

______________________________________________

______________________________________________

2. **Why were the sleep study participants sometimes given mild late-night meals?**

______________________________________________

______________________________________________

3. **Summarize Dr. Science's response to *Sleepless in Secaucus*.**

______________________________________________

______________________________________________

**READ THE PLAYBILL** Think about how the information in the playbill is arranged.

StageOne Productions
*presents*

# Oklahoma!

**Book by**
Oscar Hammerstein II

**Music by**
Richard Rodgers

**Lyrics by**
Oscar Hammerstein II

Based on the play *Green Grow the Lilacs* by Lynn Riggs

***Starring***

Robert Brown
Mieka Morioka
Badra Owens
Tiffany Pielman
Celina Rodriguez
Zack Wallace

***Also with***

Tabitha Brown
Leslie Doherty
Raul Espinosa
Heather Gold
Reggie Hamner
Willis Hitchens
Maria Jose Peña
James Siliman
Paula Tish

**Settings by**
Lina Owens

**Costumes by**
Bradley Archer

**Lighting by**
Kalani Faralan

**Sound by**
Jonna McCarthy

**Choreography by**
Agnes De Mille

**Directed by**
Layne Tish

**STRATEGY PRACTICE** Why are the actors in the musical listed in two different sections on the playbill?

**SKILL PRACTICE** Read the item. Write your response.

1. Name the songwriter(s) for *Oklahoma!* How did you determine this information?

2. Where would you find the name of a person who has a minor singing or acting role in this musical?

3. How did Agnes De Mille contribute to this production?

**READ THE PASSAGE** Think of a question about the topic of Bigfoot. As you read, look for the answer.

## Ray Wallace's Bigfoot Hoax

For decades, people have heard about sightings of a gigantic creature in the forests of the Pacific Northwest. According to the stories, the creature always left huge footprints. A logger named Ray Wallace helped popularize these stories about the creature known as Bigfoot.

In 1958, one of Wallace's workers told a newspaper about spotting the creature's tracks. Wallace explained that his workers were scared of the beast. The story spread, and some people connected the creature to other legendary monsters, especially the Abominable Snowman, or Yeti, said to live in the mountains of Nepal. Wallace had pictures and film footage of a huge furry primate to back up his story. He also tried to sell castings of giant footprints and recordings of the creature's cries.

But in 2002, after Ray Wallace died, his family members had their own story to tell. They said that Wallace was a prankster and made the giant footprints himself. Wallace's wife admitted dressing up in a Bigfoot costume as part of the hoax. Apparently, Ray Wallace enjoyed fooling people. He told his Bigfoot stories for decades. However, Wallace certainly was not responsible for all the other reported sightings of Bigfoot. In fact, some people continue to report seeing the monster. Despite some people's belief that Bigfoot exists, when Ray Wallace passed away, his own son said, "Bigfoot is dead."

**STRATEGY PRACTICE** Write a question you have about the passage. Then write the answer you found.

**SKILL PRACTICE** Read the item. Write your response.

1. What is the author's purpose for writing this text?

2. How does the author allow for the possibility that Bigfoot is real?

3. Why did the author include the quotation from Wallace's son at the end of the text?

**READ THE PASSAGE** Think of one question you have about each paragraph.

## Ephesus

Although tourists might think the best place to view Roman ruins would be the modern city of Rome, they would be mistaken. There is one city that helps visitors understand better than any other what it must have been like to live in the ancient Roman world. That city, in western Turkey, is Ephesus (EF-ih-sus). In Ephesus, visitors find fabulous ruins from around AD 100, such as the magnificent library and a theater that once seated 24,000 audience members. The ruins are among the best-preserved in the world and include houses, temples, and baths. Tourists can also visit ancient residences, complete with marble floors and frescoes painted on the walls.

Ephesus used to serve as an important trading center for the Roman Empire because it had access to the Aegean Sea. However, the river that led to the Aegean filled with silt, and today Ephesus is miles inland. The city was deserted in the Middle Ages. Visitors to Ephesus can walk down a Roman road and see buildings that the ancient Romans saw. They can appreciate feats of engineering that are still impressive, such as the incredible acoustics in the huge open-air theater. Here, Roman audience members once listened to classical plays and watched gladiators fight. At Ephesus today, tourists can experience the ancient Roman Empire in its most inspiring form.

**STRATEGY PRACTICE** Write a question you thought of while reading the first paragraph.

---

---

**SKILL PRACTICE** Read the item. Write your response.

1. What is the author's opinion of Ephesus? Cite text evidence in your response.

---

---

2. What can you learn about the Roman Empire by visiting Ephesus?

---

---

3. Is this text written to entertain, inform, or persuade? Explain your response.

---

---

**READ THE PASSAGE** Think of a question that can be answered with information from the passage.

## Taking Action

At Seven Oaks Middle School, Daniela Carrera was searching for a club to join. There was a dance club, a choir, an exercise club, and an action club that found creative ways to raise money for other people. Daniela was thinking about joining the dance club because she loved dancing.

Then Daniela's friend Ciara told her about the action club's new project. At first, Daniela was skeptical. "Why would people in a nursing home want a video-game console?" she asked Ciara.

"This would be a specific kind of console that plays fitness games. The games help people who need to exercise and move around but who can't get to a gym or exercise safely outdoors. Besides, everybody loves video games, don't they?" Ciara replied.

"Not my great-grandmother," Daniela said, laughing. But she agreed to go to the club meeting the next day.

At the meeting, Mr. Washington, the club's advisor, explained to Daniela and the others how fitness video games help motivate people to move. He described how the consoles can even help distract people who suffer from severe pain. That was all Daniela needed to hear.

"How can I help?" she asked as she signed up for the club.

"We're selling raffle tickets. With the money we raise, we'll buy two fitness consoles. We'll give one to the winner of the raffle. We'll give the other console to the nursing home," explained Mr. Washington.

"Great! Let's get started. I'm motivated to sell some tickets today!" said Daniela.

**STRATEGY PRACTICE** Write a question about information from the passage. Then ask a partner to answer it.

______________________________

**SKILL PRACTICE** Read the item. Write your response.

1. How does the action club differ from the other clubs that Daniela has considered joining?

______________________________

______________________________

2. What is the author's purpose for writing this text?

______________________________

______________________________

3. Why is one console going to the student who wins the raffle?

______________________________

______________________________

**READ THE PASSAGE** Ask yourself questions to make sure you understand what you read.

## The Smilodon and the Tiger

Although the now-extinct smilodon is also known as the saber-toothed tiger, it was not a close relative of the modern tiger. The more scientists study the two big cats, the more differences they find.

Tigers travel by themselves and run fast while chasing their prey. The smilodon, on the other hand, probably lived in packs. With much shorter tails than today's tigers, the smilodon did not have the balance to run at top speeds. It probably caught its prey by hiding quietly until an animal came near. Then the smilodon would surprise its prey.

Another main difference between today's tiger and the smilodon is the size of the smilodon's teeth. It is known as a "saber-toothed" cat because of two enormous teeth that grew from the top of its jaw. These teeth grew up to seven inches (18 cm) long and were surprisingly fragile. The smilodon probably used the teeth to bite into soft parts of its prey's body, such as its stomach. A modern tiger's teeth are much smaller, but they are stronger.

The smilodon lived in North and South America from about two million years ago until about ten thousand years ago. Tigers, of course, still exist today and live in eastern and southeastern Asia. No one knows for sure why the smilodon became extinct. However, scientists do know that many of today's tiger species are in danger of becoming extinct because of loss of habitat and human activity.

**STRATEGY PRACTICE** Write a question you had while reading. If you learned the answer, write it down.

______________________________________________

______________________________________________

**SKILL PRACTICE** Read the item. Write your response.

1. What is the author's purpose for writing this text?

______________________________________________

______________________________________________

2. Name three similarities between smilodons and modern tigers.

______________________________________________

______________________________________________

3. Name three ways in which smilodons and modern tigers differ.

______________________________________________

______________________________________________

**READ THE PASSAGE** Write questions about the parts of the passage you find difficult to understand.

## Exercise and Endurance

Endurance is the body's physical ability to do an exercise for an extended period of time. The more endurance you have, the longer you can do the exercise. Endurance is about time, as opposed to strength, which measures your power against resistance, such as weights. Athletes build up endurance by training. They plan their exercise ahead of time. Then they gradually increase the amount of exercise. For example, some people increase it a little more every week.

Exercise can strengthen your heart and other muscles. There are two main types of endurance: cardiovascular endurance and muscular endurance. Cardiovascular endurance is the ability of your heart and lungs to pump blood filled with oxygen to your muscles and the rest of your body. Oxygen acts as a fuel for your muscles to help them work better. Muscular endurance is how continuously your muscles can work without getting tired out.

Your body needs more than just oxygen to fuel itself and build endurance. Water is one kind of fuel. Food is another. Food provides energy, which is measured in calories. Your body needs energy to work. Even breathing requires energy. Your body needs even more energy when you exercise.

You do not have to be an athlete to build physical endurance. Anyone can do it! Doing exercise on a regular basis and slowly increasing the amount of time you exercise will build endurance. Endurance isn't important only for sporting events. It can help you do any physical activity longer and more easily, including activities that we do in our daily lives.

**STRATEGY PRACTICE** Write a question about something that confused you in the passage. Discuss it with a partner.

________________________________________

**SKILL PRACTICE** Read the item. Write your response.

1. How is strength different from endurance?

________________________________________

________________________________________

2. Write three activities that require endurance more than strength.

________________________________________

________________________________________

3. Is the author's purpose to inform about endurance or to persuade the reader to build endurance? Explain.

________________________________________

________________________________________

**READ THE PASSAGE** Pause after each paragraph and consider what that paragraph was mostly about.

## Prometheus

In ancient Greek mythology, Prometheus was a Titan, one of the most powerful gods. Yet even though he was a god, he found humans interesting. Zeus, the ruler of all the gods, did not care about human struggles, but Prometheus wanted to help mortals.

According to the myths, Prometheus looked for ways to help humans solve their problems. For example, he taught people how to make bricks to build homes, how to tell the seasons by looking at the stars, and how to navigate their ships. Humans, with the help of Prometheus's knowledge, began to advance. They became more independent.

Zeus ordered Prometheus not to help the humans, but Prometheus continued. After Prometheus stole fire from Zeus and gave it to people, Zeus grew incredibly angry. Until then, Zeus alone had controlled fire. By giving it to the humans, Prometheus was offering them the final power they needed to grow and prosper without the help of the gods.

Zeus was furious. "You dared to defy me?" cried Zeus. "You brought fire to those too foolish to use it properly. Now you must be punished!" Zeus chained Prometheus to a mountain and kept him bound there for years.

Finally, Heracles, a brave warrior and one of Zeus's sons, could no longer stand to see Prometheus suffer. Heracles set Prometheus free.

**SKILL PRACTICE** Read the item. Write your response.

1. Summarize this myth in one sentence.

___

___

2. Why and how did Zeus punish Prometheus?

___

___

3. What would have happened to Prometheus if Heracles had not taken action? Write your prediction.

___

___

**STRATEGY PRACTICE** Summarize what you learned about Prometheus for a partner.

**READ THE PASSAGE** Look for details that support each paragraph's main idea.

## A Diagnosis

Every Sunday at exactly 11:00 AM, my whole family gathers in the lobby of the Oak Valley Manor for Senior Citizens. That's when my parents, my brother Phillip, and I join my great-grandmother June for Sunday brunch, a spectacular buffet of omelets, pancakes, French toast, and all the other foods people don't usually have time to prepare or get to eat during the school week.

Something different about Sunday brunch lately was the change in Dr. Shepard, a friend of my great-grandma, who eats brunch with us. When I first met Dr. Shepard, he used a walker to get around but still stood straight and tall and always smiled. Lately he seemed to move more slowly, hunched over his walker, and rarely smiled.

Recently, our dog Scout had been tired and hadn't wanted to play. Since pets are allowed in the Manor on Sundays, we decided to bring Scout along. As we walked in, we heard someone holler, "Come, Scout!" From a nearby chair, Dr. Shepard reached out his arms. Scout ran to him, her tail wagging wildly. He scratched behind Scout's ears and gently rubbed her belly.

"Dogs are the best!" he said. "And I should know. I used to be a vet."

"Wow, you were that kind of doctor? Maybe you can figure out what's wrong with Scout."

Dr. Shepard chuckled. "Maybe I can!" And with a huge smile he added, "Go ahead and join your family. I'll stay right here with Scout and see if I can make a diagnosis."

**SKILL PRACTICE** Read the item. Write your response.

1. What change had the narrator noticed in Dr. Shepard prior to this visit?

_______________________________________________

_______________________________________________

2. Why is Dr. Shepard so delighted to see Scout?

_______________________________________________

_______________________________________________

3. What is the main idea of this text?

_______________________________________________

_______________________________________________

**STRATEGY PRACTICE** Describe the part of the passage that was easiest for you to visualize.

_______________________________________________

_______________________________________________

**READ THE PASSAGE** Pay attention to the details of what happens in a pond and the order in which things happen.

## The World in a Pond

An ecosystem is a community of living and nonliving things that work together. Organisms, light, heat, soil, water, and the atmosphere are all parts of an ecosystem. Any alteration to an ecosystem—such as changes in temperature, the kinds of animals living there, or pollution—can affect all parts of it. This can be especially obvious in the small, enclosed ecosystem of a pond.

In a pond, sunlight helps tiny plants called algae grow. Algae release oxygen, which fish need in order to breathe. Algae are also food for other tiny organisms. Fish eat the organisms and give off carbon dioxide, which plants use to grow.

Imagine what would happen, however, if something changed in the pond. For example, if sunlight didn't reach the pond because of thick pollution, or if the temperature of the water grew colder or warmer, the algae wouldn't grow. Without algae, there would first be less oxygen. Tiny organisms would starve. Fish would then die from the lack of oxygen. Plants would die without the carbon dioxide that fish give off. Then larger animals that eat the plants and smaller animals would not get enough food. Even humans, who eat the plants, fish, and larger animals, would feel the impact. The whole ecosystem would suffer.

**SKILL PRACTICE** Read the item. Write your response.

1. If algae stopped growing in a pond, what living thing would be the first affected?

_______________________________________________

_______________________________________________

2. How would the decline of tiny organisms affect fish?

_______________________________________________

_______________________________________________

3. How are pond plants dependent upon fish?

_______________________________________________

_______________________________________________

**STRATEGY PRACTICE** Make a numbered list telling the sequence of events that occur after algae disappear from a pond.

_______________________________________________

_______________________________________________

_______________________________________________

_______________________________________________

**READ THE PASSAGE** Pay attention to the dates and events described in the passage.

## The Cliff Dwellers

Mesa Verde, which means "green table" in Spanish, is a high plateau in Colorado. Made of sandstone and shale, this plateau rises almost 2,000 feet (610 m) above surrounding land. The mesa has many canyons with streams and rivers running through them. At the tops of the rocky canyon walls, there are many overhangs and cave-like alcoves that have formed from water seeping into the sandstone.

People first came to Mesa Verde sometime around AD 550. These early inhabitants dug into the floors of the alcoves, creating what are now called pit houses. Around AD 750, people moved out of the pit houses in the canyon walls and built above-ground houses from mud and stone. Then, around the year 1200, they returned to the alcoves in the canyon walls.

Nobody knows why the people returned to the cliff pit houses. They may have feared attack from other groups and believed the alcoves offered better protection. They may have wanted better shelter from the wind and blistering sun. Whatever the reason, the cliff dwellers stayed less than a hundred years in the pit houses after they had moved back.

By 1300, the cliff dwellings had been abandoned, probably because of a severe drought in the area. It wasn't until over four hundred years later that cowboys, trappers, and prospectors began to visit and photograph Mesa Verde, astonished by the sight of hundreds of cliff houses built into the walls of the canyons.

**SKILL PRACTICE** Read the item. Write your response.

1. Describe the types of homes that the first Mesa Verde inhabitants created.

_______________________________________________

_______________________________________________

2. When did the Mesa Verde people leave their above-ground homes and where did they go?

_______________________________________________

_______________________________________________

3. When and why do archaeologists think that Mesa Verde inhabitants left the area?

_______________________________________________

_______________________________________________

**STRATEGY PRACTICE** Describe how you visualized the cliff dwellings of the Mesa Verde people.

_______________________________________________

_______________________________________________

**READ THE PASSAGE** Think about the main events described in the passage and when they happened.

## Marching to the Sea

On March 12, 2005, several hundred people marched 240 miles (386 km) from the city of Ahmedabad (AH-mud-uh-BAHD) to the village of Dandi on the seacoast of India. They were reenacting Mahatma Gandhi's Salt March of 1930. Gandhi was an Indian whose nonviolent protests, or civil disobedience, led to India's independence from Great Britain. His program of civil disobedience began with the Salt March.

In 1930, India was a colony of Great Britain. The British had imposed a tax on salt in India to raise money. Salt was vitally important to Indians of every class and income level because it helped them preserve food and stay healthy in the country's intense heat. Gandhi and 78 followers decided to protest the tax by walking 240 miles (386 km) to the sea.

The journey lasted 23 days. Every town Gandhi passed emptied as the inhabitants ran out to watch the march. By the time Gandhi reached the sea, thousands of people had joined him. People all over India bought and sold salt illegally. The protests grew to include peaceful defiance of other laws and taxes. Gandhi was arrested and jailed by the British, but he had achieved his goal of bringing the plight of India to the world's attention. He had also started the movement that, 17 years later, would end in India becoming an independent nation.

**SKILL PRACTICE** Read the item. Write your response.

1. Write the main idea of the text in a single sentence.

______________________________

______________________________

2. What happened to Gandhi at the end of the march?

______________________________

______________________________

3. Which detail in the text lets the reader know that the Indian people supported Gandhi?

______________________________

______________________________

**STRATEGY PRACTICE** What was the reason for Gandhi's Salt March to the sea?

______________________________

______________________________

**READ THE PASSAGE** Look for the effects of wildfires listed in the passage.

## Wildfires in Washington

Wildfires take place with alarming frequency in the drier areas of the United States, especially in the western states. Not only do the fires cause immediate damage by killing plants and animals in their path, but they can also have long-term effects that harm the ecosystem.

At the Hanford Reach National Monument in Washington State, different types of wildlife—such as the burrowing owl, the sagebrush vole, and the pygmy rabbit—abound. Visitors to Hanford Reach might also see elk, porcupines, and jack rabbits that live near the free-flowing Columbia River. The area is protected from development, which has helped these species thrive.

Over the last decade, several major wildfires have broken out at Hanford Reach. Thousands of acres have burned. One type of plant that has been severely damaged in the fires is sagebrush. This poses special problems for many of the species living in the park. First, animals such as the sage grouse depend on sagebrush as part of their natural habitat. It can take thirty years for sagebrush to grow large enough to provide shelter for these animals. Second, after the sagebrush burns, an invasive species called cheat grass can grow quickly in its place. Unfortunately, cheat grass burns more easily and at higher temperatures than sagebrush. That means that after sagebrush is destroyed, wildfires can occur more frequently and be even more devastating.

**SKILL PRACTICE** Read the item. Write your response.

1. How are species protected at the Hanford Reach National Monument?

_______________________________________________

_______________________________________________

2. What is the biggest issue facing animals that survive a wildfire?

_______________________________________________

_______________________________________________

3. How does cheat grass pose a problem after a wildfire?

_______________________________________________

_______________________________________________

**STRATEGY PRACTICE** Write a sentence explaining why sagebrush is such an important plant at Hanford Reach National Monument.

_______________________________________________

_______________________________________________

**READ THE PASSAGE** Think about the problem that Phil and Curtis face and what causes it.

## Building a House of Cards

One day after school, Phil and Curtis were thinking of something fun to do. "Let's have a contest to see who can build the tallest house of cards," Phil suggested.

"Okay," said Curtis, "but you know I'm the house-of-cards champion."

"We'll see," Phil said as he took two packs of cards from his desk.

The two boys began working. Curtis first placed two cards so that they were touching each other at the top, making the shape of an upside-down V. Then he did the same thing with two more cards, placing them beside the first pair. Soon, he had a line of cards that looked like teepees. Next, he placed cards flat across the tops of the teepees to make the foundation for the next level.

Phil stood four cards on their edges to form a tall rectangle. Then he placed cards flat on top of the rectangle to make the foundation for his next level.

Now the brothers' troubles began. When Curtis tried to build his second level of teepees, he found that the cards on the bottom level would not stand. His teepees collapsed! When Phil tried to build his second level, the rectangle-shaped hut made of cards fell in a heap.

"Well, this is frustrating," said Phil.

"I have an idea," said Curtis. "Maybe my teepees would work better on top of your rectangle."

"Let's try it!" Phil said.

**SKILL PRACTICE** Read the item. Write your response.

1. Why did Phil and Curtis build houses with playing cards?

______________________________

______________________________

2. What happened when Curtis started building his second level?

______________________________

______________________________

3. What occurred after both brothers had difficulty creating their house of cards?

______________________________

______________________________

**STRATEGY PRACTICE** Write a question you had about what was happening in the passage. If you found the answer, write it.

______________________________

______________________________

**READ THE PASSAGE** Pay attention to the author's evidence for how hoodoos formed in the region.

## Hoodoos in Bryce Canyon

Imagine the spires at the top of a sand castle—the kind you create by dripping layers of very wet sand. Hoodoos, a type of rock formation found primarily in Bryce Canyon, Utah, look something like wet sand, but they are made from colorful rock. Every year, millions of people come to Bryce Canyon to look at the pole-shaped hoodoos, which range from 5 to 150 feet (1.5 to 46 m) tall.

What caused these amazing formations? Scientists believe that water is responsible. Over millions of years, water and ice have shaped the limestone of the area, creating canyons, deep bowls, plateaus, and hoodoos. On many days in this region, the temperatures are freezing at night and much warmer during the day. The sun melts snow, and the resulting water flows into cracks in the limestone. When the water freezes at night, it expands and causes the cracks to widen and pull the rock apart. This is called frost wedging. Another way that water shapes the hoodoos is simply through rainfall. The rain contains a small amount of acid, which causes the soft limestone to dissolve. Some layers of rock in the hoodoos are harder than other layers, making parts of the hoodoos wear away more slowly. This gives hoodoos their unusual shapes and appearances.

Visitors to Bryce Canyon can hike through miles of natural mazes formed by hoodoos. However, to protect the fragile spires, visitors are asked to stay on the trails. If they were to climb on the hoodoos, they could damage the formations and rob future generations of the chance to see something that took eons to form.

**SKILL PRACTICE** Read the item. Write your response.

1. Why did the author mention sand castle spires at the beginning of the text?

______________________________

______________________________

2. *Hoodoos can form from very hard rock such as granite.* Prove this statement true or false using evidence from the text.

______________________________

______________________________

3. Can humans affect hoodoos? Use quotation marks to cite text evidence in your response.

______________________________

**STRATEGY PRACTICE** What information from the passage would be important for writing a report about weathering in Bryce Canyon?

______________________________

______________________________

**READ THE PASSAGE** Look for the evidence that the author gives to support each claim she makes.

## The Value of Gold

People have treasured gold for thousands of years. But just what makes gold so valuable? Gold has several important properties that contribute to its value. First, it reflects light very well and has an attractive yellow color, making it ideal for use in jewelry. Second, it is very malleable, or easy to shape. Because gold is soft and easy to work with, it can be hammered into thin sheets that do not crack. These sheets can then be used to add decorative details to artwork or buildings. Third, it does not rust or wear away. It keeps its shape, which means that gold jewelry and art objects can pass from generation to generation and become more valuable over time. Fourth, gold is an excellent conductor of electricity, making it a good choice for electronics.

One of the most important reasons that gold is valuable, however, is that it is rare. Although gold exists in many places throughout the world, it is not easy to find or to mine. People who mine gold usually have to work very hard to get even tiny amounts of the precious metal. The fact that it is both beautiful and useful makes people want more of this precious metal than they can easily get, which drives up its price.

Finally, gold is valuable because people perceive it to be a symbol of wealth. Throughout recorded history, gold has been associated with wealth and power. Today we still value it for many of the same reasons that our ancestors did.

**SKILL PRACTICE** Read the item. Write your response.

1. What evidence did the author use to explain why gold is ideal for use in jewelry?

_______________________________________________

_______________________________________________

2. Why are small amounts of gold commonly used in electronics?

_______________________________________________

_______________________________________________

3. Quote the statement from the text that explains the primary reason why gold is valuable.

_______________________________________________

_______________________________________________

**STRATEGY PRACTICE** Write a question that can be answered with information from the passage. Then have a partner answer the question.

_______________________________________________

_______________________________________________

**READ THE PASSAGE** Think about why the author wrote the passage and how Shirley Chisholm was important.

## Shirley Chisholm

"Aim high!" Shirley Chisholm told her political supporters, and she practiced what she preached. Born in 1924 in Brooklyn, New York, Chisholm spent part of her childhood in the island nation of Barbados. She returned to New York later, graduated from Brooklyn College, and earned a Master of Arts degree at Columbia University. Chisholm spent some time working in early childhood education before running for political office in the New York State Assembly.

After serving in the assembly, Chisholm ran for U.S. Congress in 1968 and became the first African American woman to be elected. Chisholm opposed the Vietnam War, and in her first speech in Congress, she promised to vote against any more spending on defense. "Our children, our jobless men, our deprived, rejected and starving fellows, our dejected citizens must come first," she said.

Aiming higher still, in 1972 Chisholm decided to run for president of the United States. She was the first African American to run as a candidate for the presidency in a major political party, and she was the first woman to run for president as a democrat. Ultimately, the democrats chose George McGovern as their candidate. McGovern later lost the presidential election to republican Richard Nixon. Afterward, Chisholm explained that she was tired of waiting for change to come someday in the future. "I ran because somebody had to do it first. I ran because most people thought the country was not ready for a black candidate, not ready for a woman candidate. Someday—it was time in 1972 to make that someday come."

**SKILL PRACTICE** Read the item. Write your response.

1. What two political offices did Shirley Chisholm hold?

2. Write two facts that demonstrate Chisholm's ideal of aiming high.

3. Why does the author include the quotation at the end of the text?

**STRATEGY PRACTICE** What information in the passage is most important for understanding Shirley Chisholm's political career?

**READ THE PASSAGE** Compare the eating habits of ancient Romans to how people eat today.

## Eating the Roman Way Today

It's hard to believe that there could be many similarities between the way we eat today and the diet and eating habits of ancient Romans. However, excavations at the ancient Roman towns of Pompeii and nearby Herculaneum have uncovered at least one significant parallel. Romans enjoyed convenient ways to get their food and ate on the go, just as we do today.

Buying baked bread is one example of a convenience in both the ancient and modern worlds. Most people today purchase bread in a store. There is evidence that Romans bought their bread, too, rather than baking it themselves. A large wall painting in Pompeii shows customers buying loaves of bread in a shop. Archaeologists have identified more than 30 shops that may have been bakeries. Signs on walls told Roman shoppers that certain vendors sold bread. In addition to these discoveries, archaeologists found that few homes in Pompeii had ovens, which suggests that most people did not bake at home.

Ancient Romans also had a version of take-out food. Pompeii is filled with shops that contain dishes to hold or display food. Many shops had built-in stoves that allowed them to cook and serve food. Types of foods that have been found in these shops include dates and lentils.

Archaeologists have also uncovered many houses with small barbecue grills. However, few of these houses had sets of dishes. Taken together, these pieces of evidence suggest that Romans frequently grabbed a quick bite to eat at home, right off the grill, or bought a meal to go. Sound familiar?

**SKILL PRACTICE** Read the item. Write your response.

1. What are two ways in which ancient Romans' diets were similar to our own?

______________________________

______________________________

2. Name two ways in which ancient Romans' eating habits differ from modern ones.

______________________________

______________________________

3. What is the most surprising fact in the article? How did you choose it?

______________________________

______________________________

**STRATEGY PRACTICE** Describe a common eating habit that you share with the ancient Romans.

______________________________

______________________________

**READ THE PASSAGE** Read each account and look for how they are similar and different.

## The Whale Watch

Jeongsoo and Samuel went on a whale-watching trip to Cape Cod, Massachusetts, with their class. They each wrote an account of what they saw and did. Read their accounts.

**Jeongsoo's Account**

I had looked forward to our Cape Cod whale-watching trip all year. When we finally got on the boat, I thought, "This is it!" After a year of studying everything about whales, we were finally going to see them. Being on the boat was great. It was sunny and windy, the waves were enormous, and it wasn't long before we noticed our first whale, a huge finback that spouted water up through its blowhole just a few feet from the boat. We saw 12 whales altogether, including minke whales, humpbacks, and the endangered right whale. And I videotaped them all! They were the most amazing creatures I'd ever seen.

**Samuel's Account**

All year our class had studied whales, and I worked really hard learning about them and about the ocean. I could hardly wait to see the whales in their own habitat, and I was excited when we finally got to the boat. The waves were huge, though, and when the boat started moving, I began to feel weird. Then I got nauseated—really, really nauseated. I spent the whole day miserable with seasickness, curled up in a chair in the boat's cabin. I heard everyone shouting as the whales breached and spouted, but I missed it all. Luckily, Jeongsoo videotaped the whales, so I got to see his video. The whales really were awesome.

**SKILL PRACTICE** Read the item. Write your response.

1. Name two similarities between Jeongsoo's and Samuel's accounts.

_______________

_______________

2. What did Jeongsoo do that ended up helping Samuel?

_______________

_______________

3. Why was Jeongsoo's experience more enjoyable than Samuel's?

_______________

**STRATEGY PRACTICE** Are the accounts organized by cause and effect, sequence, or main idea and details? How does the organization help you compare and contrast the accounts?

_______________

_______________

**READ THE PASSAGE** Use clues from the passage to make inferences about microfinance.

## A Little Can Go a Long Way

In a village in Uganda, a woman named Fatima Serwona ran a small store. She sold food and other useful items. However, she had trouble making enough money to keep the shelves stocked. To stay in business, Fatima got a microfinance loan—a small sum of money from a person in another country. It was just enough for her to buy a cellphone. She let villagers make calls using her phone and charged them a small fee for each call. This helped her make enough money to keep her shelves stocked with items. Fatima then used the money to send her children to school and improve their lives, as well as her own.

Microfinance is the practice of giving small loans to people in need. Most microfinance loans are for less than two hundred dollars. The loans are used to start or expand a small business, such as catching fish, raising chickens, weaving, or selling produce. Lenders are willing to make these loans because most of the people who receive them are very likely to repay the loans.

Microfinance loans are important for several reasons. The businesses that these loans support often provide needed services or goods to their communities. Also, many of the people who receive microfinance loans cannot get money any other way. And although they have to pay a high rate of interest on the money they borrow, the rate is lower than if they borrowed from a local moneylender.

It doesn't seem like such a small amount of money could make a big difference, but microfinance loans have been shown to help improve individual lives and revitalize whole communities like Fatima's.

**SKILL PRACTICE** Read the item. Write your response.

1. Why did Fatima Serwona buy a cellphone?

_______________________________________________

_______________________________________________

2. Why do so many microfinance borrowers repay their loans?

_______________________________________________

_______________________________________________

3. Why do the microfinance loans come from outside Uganda?

_______________________________________________

_______________________________________________

**STRATEGY PRACTICE** If you were given a microfinance loan, what would you do with the money?

_______________________________________________

_______________________________________________

**READ THE PASSAGE** Use what you know about ecosystems and food webs to help you understand the passage.

## The Return of the Wolf

Wolves once prospered in Yellowstone National Park, but by 1926, humans had hunted them to extinction there. The absence of wolves affected many parts of the Yellowstone ecosystem. Most significantly, the disappearance of wolves led to a huge increase in the number of elk. This in turn had negative effects on plants and animals in the park.

Park authorities tried to keep the elk population under control by hunting, but in the late 1960s and 1970s, the U.S. government and the park managers began considering a new policy. They wanted to return to natural processes for regulating the balance of wildlife in the park. In 1995, Congress authorized reintroducing the gray wolf to Yellowstone. The first wolves were brought in from Canada a year later.

Almost immediately, authorities noticed differences in the park. As a result of the reintroduction of wolves, the number of elk declined. This led to an unexpected change. The number of willow trees and aspen, which elk eat, increased. Beavers, which feed on willows, in turn grew more numerous. In addition, the populations of some songbird species and small mammals that live in aspen stands have since grown. Other animals and people have benefited, too. Scavengers, or animals that eat dead animals, have increased in number. And visitors to Yellowstone are able to see and hear wolves in the park again.

**SKILL PRACTICE** Read the item. Write your response.

1. Why were there too many elk in Yellowstone National Park in the early 1990s?

2. Without wolves in the park, how and why was the vegetation at Yellowstone affected?

3. Why has the number of scavengers risen since the reintroduction of wolves?

**STRATEGY PRACTICE** Is the passage organized by compare and contrast, cause and effect, or problem and solution? Explain.

**READ THE PASSAGE** Look for the details that describe how Maria and Ellen are similar and different.

## My Scientist Hero

My name is Maria Ochoa. I'm in sixth grade. For as long as I can remember, I have been interested in space. I sleep under a ceiling of glow-in-the-dark stars. I have a poster of the solar system across from my mirror. When I grow up, I want to be an astronaut, just like Ellen Ochoa.

I first heard about Ellen Ochoa in school. How cool that the first Hispanic woman in space has the same last name as mine! We have other things in common as well. We were both born in Los Angeles, raised by one parent, and have four siblings. We even both play the flute and volleyball!

Ellen studied physics and electrical engineering in college. A few years later, she was chosen to be trained as an astronaut, but only the best become astronauts. They are taught more math, science, and technology, as well as how to live in space. For example, they learn about wearing a space suit and how to float in space when they are weightless. Ellen became an astronaut in 1991, when she had to get even more training! She had to learn things such as how to do experiments in space and go on spacewalks.

In 1993, Ellen flew to space for the first time on the shuttle *Discovery*. She told reporters that she could only imagine the pride her grandparents would feel, knowing that their granddaughter grew up to travel in space. The crew collected lots of data on how the sun affects Earth's ozone layer, which absorbs the sun's ultraviolet light. The ozone layer keeps Earth warm enough to live on; holes in the ozone are dangerous.

I want to be an astronaut scientist, too. I won't be the first Hispanic woman to leave Earth, but I hope to be the first one to land on Mars!

**SKILL PRACTICE** Read the item. Write your response.

1. How are both Maria and Ellen similar?

_______________________________________________

_______________________________________________

2. Why do you think astronaut scientists need so much extra training?

_______________________________________________

_______________________________________________

3. Name two adjectives that describe Ellen Ochoa. Explain your choices.

_______________________________________________

**STRATEGY PRACTICE** Think about what you might want to do later in life. Who is a good role model? How can that person help you work toward your goal?

_______________________________________________

_______________________________________________

**READ THE PASSAGE** Think about whom the passage is about and where the events in it take place.

## One School at a Time

Greg Mortenson is an adventurer who once loved to climb mountains. Born in 1957, he grew up on the slopes of Mt. Kilimanjaro in Tanzania, Africa. After his sister Christa died in 1992, he decided to try climbing Pakistan's K2, the second-highest mountain in the world, in her memory. Although Mt. Everest in the Himalaya Mountains is higher, K2 is considered more difficult and treacherous to climb. During an attempt to climb the mountain in 1993, snow, ice, and bad weather forced Mortenson to turn back.

Mortenson recovered from frostbite and exhaustion in the rural Pakistani village of Korphe. There he saw a group of children writing in the dirt with sticks. He learned that they had no pens or pencils, no books—not even a school or a teacher. Mortenson promised to build them a school, even though he had no idea how he would accomplish it.

It took years to raise the money to build the school. Some of the contributions to Mortenson's cause came as pennies donated by American schoolchildren. Mortenson even sold his own belongings to raise cash. The Korphe School was finished in 1996.

Since then, Mortenson has established more than 75 schools in rural Pakistan, Afghanistan, and Tajikistan. His schools educate both boys and girls in an area where schooling for girls is very rare. Mortenson's aim is to use education to promote peace in this often dangerous and violent area, one school at a time.

**SKILL PRACTICE** Read the item. Write your response.

1. How did the time Mortenson spent in Korphe change his life?

______________________________________________

______________________________________________

2. How did Mortenson's goal change between the beginning of the text and the end?

______________________________________________

______________________________________________

3. Name two nouns that apply to Greg Mortenson. Explain your choices.

______________________________________________

______________________________________________

**STRATEGY PRACTICE** How do you think Mortenson changed between 1993 and the time described at the end of the passage? How do you think the setting contributed to the change in his character?

______________________________________________

______________________________________________

**READ THE PASSAGE** Think about how the character describes his actions and the place he visited.

## The Blue Lagoon

I have always loved going to unique, out-of-the-way places, but the strangest place I've ever visited was the Blue Lagoon in Iceland. The seawater of the Blue Lagoon is heated far beneath Earth's surface. Although most lagoons are natural, this one is man-made. A nearby power plant pumps the hot water up from a mile (1.6 km) below the surface, through a lava formation. The water that's not used to make heat and electricity at the power plant is sent into the huge lagoon cut out of solid black rock formed from lava. The water is very warm—about 104°F (40°C). It's also full of minerals that make it appear a bright, shockingly blue color.

When I visited, I walked along a pathway carved through rock, toward a bathhouse. There, I changed into a swimsuit and ran outside. The air was freezing, so I plunged into the lagoon, shivering. In a minute I was warm—except for the top of my head, which was out of the water. Clouds of steam rose into the chilly air above the water so thickly that I could hardly see the dozens of other people bathing. The water felt silky, and I slathered an unusual mud on my face from wooden tubs around the lagoon. I rinsed the mud off under a hot waterfall. By the time I left, I was sure I would never experience anything stranger or more wonderful than the Blue Lagoon.

**SKILL PRACTICE** Read the item. Write your response.

1. What is the setting for this text? Include as much detail as possible in your response.

___

___

2. Why was the narrator warm despite the freezing air temperature?

___

___

3. Did the narrator enjoy spending time at the Blue Lagoon? Cite text evidence in your response.

___

___

**STRATEGY PRACTICE** Write the words or phrases from the passage that helped you visualize the Blue Lagoon.

___

___

**READ THE PASSAGE** Think about the moral, or lesson, of the passage.

## The Most Powerful Thing in the World

Long ago, there lived a man who worked as a humble stonecutter. He was not happy with his job or his position in life. As he struggled at his work, chipping away at stone, he saw a wealthy merchant pass by and thought, "How I wish I were as powerful and influential as that merchant!" Suddenly, the stonecutter was transformed into a wealthy and powerful merchant. Others now envied him.

One hot day, as the wealthy man walked around the town observing all that he owned, he became annoyed by the strength of the sun's rays. "How I wish I were as powerful as the sun!" he thought, and suddenly he became the sun, scorching others with his heat and brilliance.

Then one day a dark cloud crossed beneath him. Rain poured down and the wind blew, limiting the sun's power over others. "How I wish I were as powerful as the storm!" he thought, and he became a storm with rain and wind. People feared his great force, but when he blew against a huge rock, the rock did not move. "How I wish I were as powerful as that rock!" he thought, and in a moment he became the rock.

Not long afterward, he heard a hammering sound and felt a part of himself change. "What could be more powerful than me, the rock?" he wondered. He looked down and saw, much to his surprise and disappointment, that a humble stonecutter was chipping away at him.

**SKILL PRACTICE** Read the item. Write your response.

1. What is the theme of this text?

______________________________

______________________________

2. Why is the stonecutter eventually unhappy with each of his transformations?

______________________________

______________________________

3. What will probably happen next? Explain your reasoning.

______________________________

______________________________

**STRATEGY PRACTICE** If the stonecutter had stopped making wishes after he became a merchant, how would it have affected the passage's theme?

______________________________

______________________________

______________________________

**READ THE PASSAGE** Think about how the author feels about animals and people working together.

## Helping Horses

Many people with visual impairment use guide dogs to help them get safely from place to place and to alert them to danger. But what can blind people do if they are allergic to dogs or just don't like them? For some people, the answer is provided by the Guide Horse Foundation.

Janet and Don Burleson founded the nonprofit organization in 1999. They began training miniature horses to help guide visually impaired people. Miniature horses look just like regular horses, only much smaller. They are generally less than 34 inches (86 cm) tall.

Cuddles was the foundation's first guide horse in full service. She became 45-year-old Dan Shaw's helper. Shaw has an eye disease that caused his sight to deteriorate. One night, while filling out an application to get a guide dog, Shaw heard a news story on TV about people training horses to guide the blind. Shaw loves horses and wanted a guide animal that would live a long time. He applied, and a year later, Cuddles and Shaw began training as a team.

On a trip to New York, Cuddles helped Shaw safely navigate Times Square, a very busy part of the city at night. The next day, Cuddles calmly rode the elevator with Shaw to the crowded top of the Empire State Building, a famous skyscraper. Cuddles even guided Shaw on the ferry ride to the Statue of Liberty, rode the escalator in a store, and traveled on the subway system.

Shaw says that he feels truly blessed to have Cuddles. He believes that Cuddles has changed his life for the better by giving him more independence and self-reliance.

**SKILL PRACTICE** Read the item. Write your response.

1. How are guide horses and guide dogs similar?

_______________________________________________

_______________________________________________

2. Describe two qualities that are important in a guide horse. Explain why each quality is essential.

_______________________________________________

_______________________________________________

3. How did people probably react when they saw Shaw and Cuddles in New York City?

_______________________________________________

_______________________________________________

**STRATEGY PRACTICE** Describe how you visualized Cuddles and Dan Shaw on the city streets.

_______________________________________________

_______________________________________________

**READ THE PASSAGE** Think about whom the passage is about and what the theme of the story is.

## A Musical Prodigy

Imagine knowing at age two what you want to do for the rest of your life. Jay Greenberg, nicknamed "Bluejay" because these birds make a lot of noise for their size, did just that. He has been called the greatest musical talent to come along in 200 years. And all of this praise was said about a teenager!

When Greenberg was just two years old, he started drawing pictures of musical instruments and wrote the word *cello*. His parents got him a cello, and by age three, he was composing music. In 2001, at age ten, he began attending the Juilliard School, one of the world's best music conservatories, in New York City. Within two years, he had composed five symphonies. And by 2009, he had written more than 70 musical compositions for such groups as the New Haven Symphony and the London Symphony Orchestra.

Greenberg is a musical prodigy, or extremely gifted young person. Unlike most kids, he doesn't download music from the Internet; he downloads it from his own mind! When he composes works, he hears them in his head complete, as if an orchestra were playing them. His hero is Beethoven, and for fun, he fools around with classical music compositions, changing and rewriting them. He is completely devoted to his calling, once telling his mother that he would die if he could not compose music.

**SKILL PRACTICE** Read the item. Write your response.

1. What is the theme of this text?

______________________________________________

______________________________________________

2. Name two achievements that made it clear that Greenberg was a musical prodigy.

______________________________________________

______________________________________________

3. When do you think Greenberg's parents first realized that he was extremely talented?

______________________________________________

______________________________________________

**STRATEGY PRACTICE** What information in the passage helps you understand why Jay Greenberg is called a prodigy?

______________________________________________

______________________________________________

**READ THE PASSAGE** Think about why the author wrote the passage.

## Don't Cut the Arts

Has the number of art classes at your school been reduced? Did your school cancel next year's play? Have band classes been eliminated? When school budgets are under pressure, the arts always seem to be the first programs that are cut. Classes in painting, drama, dance, and music—as well as after-school arts activities—are often the first to go.

Some people believe that arts funding should be cut. They claim that school performance is measured by standardized test scores, not by a successful arts program. So why shouldn't schools cut arts programs when money is tight?

According to the National Governors' Association (NGA), there are many reasons to preserve the arts in schools. Students exposed to the arts have higher academic achievement and are better at planning and working toward goals. Students who study the arts are:

- four times more likely to get academic awards or win a writing award;
- four times more likely to take part in a math or science fair; and
- more likely to score higher in creative thinking, fluency, and originality.

In their report "The Impact of Arts Education on Workforce Preparation," the governors also observe that schools with strong arts programs have:

- significantly fewer discipline problems;
- less absenteeism; and
- lower dropout rates.

Should we cut the arts in times of economic difficulty? This author says "No!"

**SKILL PRACTICE** Read the item. Write your response.

1. What is the author's purpose for writing this text?

_______________________________________________

_______________________________________________

2. Why did the author use bulleted lists?

_______________________________________________

_______________________________________________

3. Why did the author quote the National Governors' Association in this text?

_______________________________________________

**STRATEGY PRACTICE** Write one question you had while reading the passage. If you found the answer, write it, too.

_______________________________________________

_______________________________________________

**READ THE PASSAGE** Think about why the author wrote the passage and what it is mostly about.

## Harvesting Rain the Easy Way

As people in the American Southwest become concerned about long periods of drought, many are rediscovering water-harvesting techniques from ancient times. Water harvesting is the capturing, moving, and storing of rainwater for later use, often in landscaping. Rain barrels attached to a roof's downspouts are one low-tech way of harvesting rainwater, but an even simpler and cheaper method is to build *swales* and *berms*.

What are swales? Swales are simply depressions, or low areas, in the ground. They allow rainwater to stay put for a while so that it can soak into the soil. This enables fruit trees, vegetable gardens, and landscape plants to use it as needed. And berms? Berms are raised areas that direct water into swales.

One simple way to create berms and swales is to dig a hole in the soil about a foot deep and pile up that same dirt to create a berm around it. The dirt is then pounded down to form a sturdy wall around the swale. Doing this over and over can create a whole network of berms and swales. Boomerang-shaped berms can direct water toward trees or other plants. Repeating serpentine-shaped berms can provide the water needed to turn a barren slope into a beautiful garden. And it's easier than you think. Once again, a low-tech approach works just fine! Just gather your friends, provide plenty of lemonade and music, and have a swale-stomping dance party in your yard.

**SKILL PRACTICE** Read the item. Write your response.

1. What is the author's purpose for writing this text?

2. Does the author think that berms and swales are useful for irrigation? Cite text evidence in your response.

3. What possible problem can you foresee with the use of swales?

**STRATEGY PRACTICE** Explain why some people, according to the author, are concerned about conserving fresh water. Is this a concern where you live?

**READ THE PASSAGE** Look for clues in the passage that help you figure out what will happen next.

## The Dog Hoser

The United States has been the birthplace of thousands of important inventions, from the incandescent light bulb to the computer mouse. However, the U.S. has also seen the birth of thousands of wacky and even ridiculous inventions. One example of an odd invention is the dog hoser.

Grooming a dog at home can be difficult. Many dog owners don't have the tools or knowledge needed to properly cut an animal's fur. For these reasons, some dog owners take their animals to professional groomers for haircuts. After groomers cut a dog's fur, they often use a vacuum cleaner to remove the cut fur from the pet's coat. This is where the real trouble starts. Many dogs are terrified of the strange machine and its scary noise.

To solve the problem, one creative inventor designed a vacuum cleaner dogs might actually like. The dog hoser is a vacuum cleaner that looks just like a dog.

Dog-shaped, with a vacuum cleaner hidden in its belly, the dog hoser looks like a furry pal. Its sound is muffled, and the hose is disguised as the dog's tail. It may look like a new friend, but what do you think happens when the groomer pulls out the dog hoser's tail and starts sweeping it across the dog's body?

After trying one in his shop, one dog groomer said, "My client's expensive poodle cowered in fear when I used it." A month later, the client reported that her dog was still afraid of interacting with other dogs.

**SKILL PRACTICE** Read the item. Write your response.

1. Does the dog hoser cut into professional dog groomers' business? Defend your stance.

2. What do you predict will happen with the dog hoser invention?

3. Why did the author include a quote from a dog groomer?

**STRATEGY PRACTICE** Write a question about information from the passage. Then ask a partner to answer it.

**READ THE PASSAGE** Use clues from the passage to predict what will likely happen next to the California condor.

## Back from the Brink of Extinction

The California condor is not a handsome bird. Its featherless scalp is a shocking pink-orange. Its feeding habits—feasting on the flesh of dead animals—should not be mentioned at the dinner table. So why do naturalists at Arizona's Grand Canyon want to protect this bird?

These huge vultures were once found across North America from Mexico to Canada. But by 1982, only 22 existed in the world and the species faced extinction. By 1985, only nine California condors remained.

Because the loss of one species can affect a whole ecosystem, naturalists sprang into action. They decided to capture the remaining condors to begin a captive breeding program. As females produced eggs, some eggs were removed and raised by people, using a hand puppet that looked like a condor head. This was done to keep chicks from imprinting on humans, or thinking humans were their parents. Naturalists wanted the chicks to feel safe with other condors, not with humans.

The captive population increased dramatically. Then, beginning in 1992, newly bred chicks were released into the wild. In 1996, two males and four females were released 30 miles north of the Grand Canyon. In 2004, the first condor that had been hatched and raised in Arizona in more than a century took flight. Although it died in 2006, others have since hatched and taken flight. Today, around 80 California condors soar majestically above northern Arizona's canyon country.

**SKILL PRACTICE** Read the item. Write your response.

1. What would probably have happened to the condors without the captive breeding program?

2. What might occur if a condor chick imprinted on a human?

3. Predict what is likely to happen to the California condor in the future.

**STRATEGY PRACTICE** What other animals do the California condors remind you of? Why?

**READ THE PASSAGE** Think about why the author wrote the passage, and use the clues in the passage to predict what will likely happen next.

## A Wild Flamingo Chase

Rodney read the headline in the local paper: "Flamingo Flocks to Fern Fields." An exotic bird had found its way to his small California town. It was a flamingo, the report said, a real one—not like the faded plastic version planted in Rodney's neighbor's yard. The town didn't even have a zoo, so this news was really exciting. But where was the bird? Rodney thought it would stick out like a sore thumb.

Only one man in town claimed to have seen the wild bird, in a wetland park on the outskirts of town. He described the flamingo's pink feathers and said it stood approximately 3 feet (0.9 m) tall. He also said the flamingo did not seem sick or hurt.

Rodney thought the story sounded suspicious, though, so he decided to go on a flamingo-finding expedition. He also decided to take his best friend, Paul, with him. "If we find it," Rodney said, "we can write a report on protecting wild species." The boys assembled their gear—tall rubber boots, binoculars, and a camera. They packed some peanut butter sandwiches, too. Then they set out for the wetlands.

With boots up to their thighs, Rodney and Paul trudged through muck and mud for what seemed like an eternity, but they never spotted the flamingo. Finally the sun began to set, and a cold wind cut through the boys' jackets. Rodney and Paul decided to head home.

As they turned onto Paul's dark street, they saw Paul's mom waiting on the porch. Paul dragged his feet up the driveway. His mother put her arm on his shoulder, and the two went inside.

Rodney continued down the street toward his house, past his neighbor's yard and that ridiculous plastic pink flamingo. "Great," Rodney thought, "now they have a pair." Out of the corner of his eye, Rodney saw something move.

**SKILL PRACTICE** Read the item. Write your response.

1. What is the author's purpose for writing this text?

2. What will Paul probably tell his mother?

3. What is apt to happen next? How do you know?

**STRATEGY PRACTICE** Write a question you thought of while you read the passage.

**READ THE GLOSSARY** Pay attention to the important features on the page.

## African Instrument Glossary

**Mbila:** (m-BIL-uh) A wooden xylophone played by striking planks with a rubber mallet. Shells mounted under the wooden boards amplify the sounds. These instruments can be several feet long and can be played by two or more musicians at one time. (Origin: Mozambique)

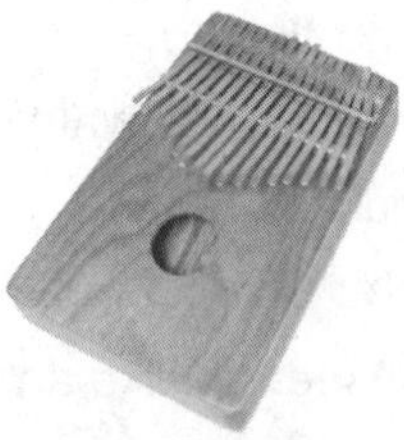

**Mbira:** (m-BIR-uh) A hand-held piano with 22 to 28 metal keys attached to a wooden board that amplifies the sounds made by plucking the keys with the thumbs. Modern mbiras often use recycled materials for the keys, such as furniture springs or bicycle spokes. Bottle caps, shells, or other objects are attached to the wooden board. They create a buzz that adds depth to the sound and increases volume. (Origin: Eastern and Southern Africa)

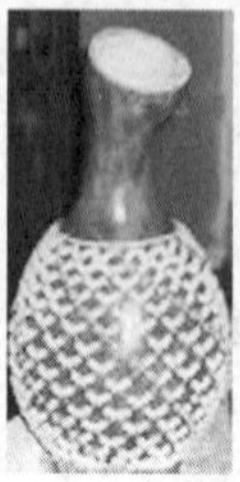

**Shekere:** (shay-KUH-ray) A percussion instrument made out of a dried gourd covered with a beaded net. Most shekeres are held in two hands. Players shake, twist, drop, or slap the instrument to create rhythmic sounds. (Origin: Nigeria)

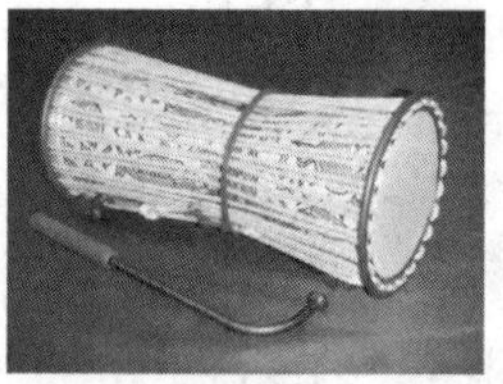

**Talking Drum:** A two-headed drum that is shaped like an hourglass and can produce a wide variety of pitches. The drum's heads are made of goat, lizard, or fish skin that is stretched over wooden hoops. The two heads are connected by leather cords. Holding the drum under one arm, the player squeezes the cords to change the drum's pitch. Notes are played by striking the heads with a special stick. The instrument is called a talking drum because it can be used to reproduce the sounds of spoken language. (Origin: Nigeria and Ghana)

**SKILL PRACTICE** Read the item. Write your response.

1. In what ways are the mbila and mbira similar?

2. Describe how a musician holds a talking drum.

3. Which instrument's name is pronounced with two long vowel sounds? How can you tell?

**STRATEGY PRACTICE** How is the first sentence in each glossary entry important?

**READ THE TABLE OF CONTENTS** Pay attention to how the table of contents is organized.

## A Beginner's Guide to Video Game Design

TABLE OF CONTENTS



**SKILL PRACTICE** Read the item. Write your response.

1. In which chapter would you look to find the definition of role-playing games?

2. If you were writing a report about how physics influences video games, to which page would turn? How do you know?

3. Explain the reasoning behind the Part Four section title.

**STRATEGY PRACTICE** Why do you think this book is divided into four parts?

**READ THE PASSAGE** Look at the information presented in the graph.

## Population Pyramids

How can you see an entire population at once? More than a quarter billion people live in the United States. That's a large number to understand, but statistics can give an overall view of the population's characteristics. A population pyramid is a graph used to show how an area's population is divided into ages and genders. Each bar in a population pyramid represents the percentage of the male or female U.S. population in a specific age range.

The shape of a population pyramid gives information about a population, too. For example, a pyramid that is wider on top than it is on the bottom means that there are more older people than young people. Reasons for this pattern might include a low birth rate, a high death rate among young people due to wars or disease, or the increase in the nation's young people moving to other countries. Similarly, a pyramid that is heavier on the bottom means there are more young people than old.

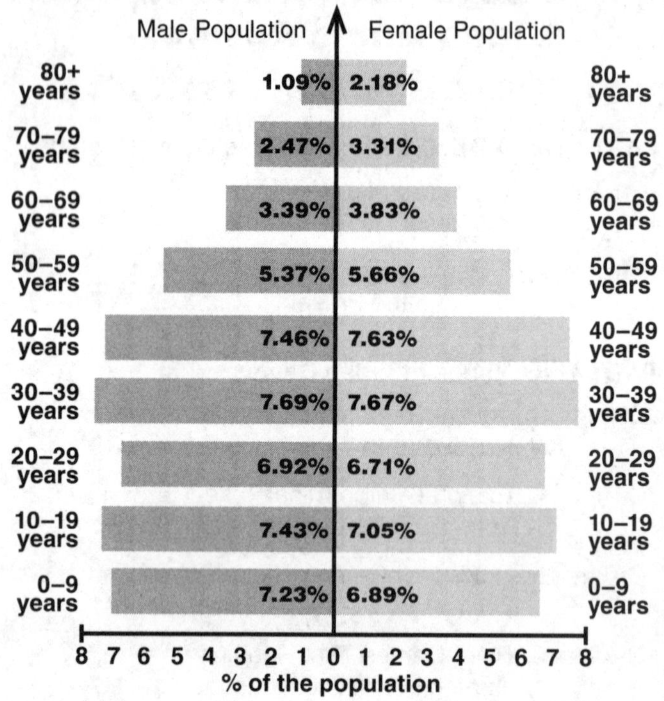

**Age Distribution in the U.S. by Gender, 2000**

**SKILL PRACTICE** Read the item. Write your response.

1. *There are more females than males in their thirties.* Use the graph to prove this statement true or false.

2. Draw a conclusion based on your comparison of the 10–19 age group with the 40–49 age group.

3. In which age group are there twice as many females as males? What are the actual percentages?

**STRATEGY PRACTICE** According to the passage, why is the shape of a population pyramid significant?

 

**READ THE PASSAGE** Think about what the information tells you.

## Top Five Languages Spoken Worldwide

There are over 6,800 distinct languages spoken on Earth. But which languages are spoken by the most people? And which language is spoken in the most countries?

According to people who study language, Mandarin is spoken by more people than any other language. It is the most common language spoken in China, which is the country with the largest population.

Although Mandarin is spoken by the greatest number of people, English is spoken in more countries than any other language. The United States has the largest English-speaking population, followed by India, Nigeria, the United Kingdom, and Germany. This includes people who speak English as a second language.

Other languages with many speakers include Hindi and Urdu, which are forms of the same language, Hindustani. They are official languages in India, Pakistan, and Fiji. Spanish is the official language in most of Latin America and South America. Arabic, which is spoken in most Middle Eastern and North African countries, is the fifth most common language. It is an official language in 16 countries.

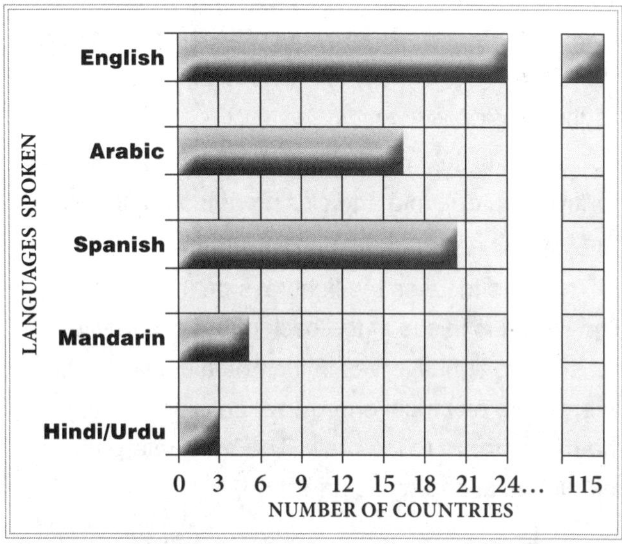


**SKILL PRACTICE** Read the item. Write your response.

1. Which language in this graph is spoken in the fewest number of countries?

2. According to the text, which country has the second-largest English-speaking population?

3. Draw a conclusion about why Mandarin is spoken by more people than English when English is spoken in 115 countries.

**STRATEGY PRACTICE** Describe how the information in the graph is organized.

**READ THE PASSAGE** Study the passage and the diagram.

## The Way We See

Light rays enter the eye through the transparent **cornea**. The rays then pass through the **pupil,** which changes size to adjust to different light levels. The pupil dilates, or becomes bigger, in dark rooms and will contract, or become smaller, in brightly lit places.

The **iris** is the colored part of the eye, and it controls the opening and closing of the pupil. Irises can be blue, green, brown, gray, or hazel.

The **lens** focuses the light rays on the retina. The **retina** is tissue at the back of the eye that is sensitive to light. Nerves in the retina convert light energy into electrical energy, which is sent along the **optic nerve** to the brain. The brain interprets the electrical energy as an image.

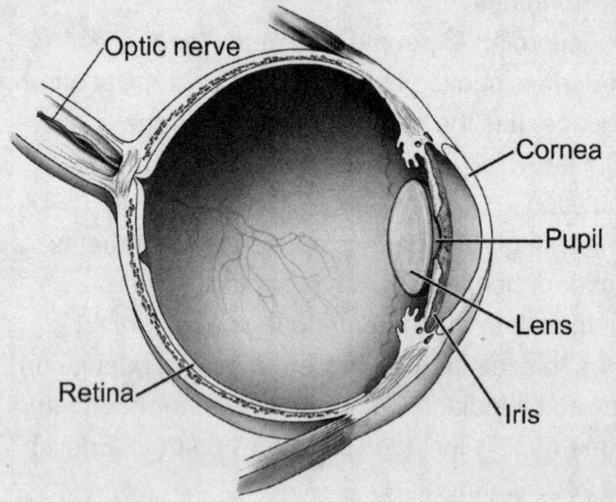


**SKILL PRACTICE** Read the item. Write your response.

1. What do the diagram labels identify?

2. Why are there boldfaced words in the text?

3. Which parts of the human eye are located behind the lens?

**STRATEGY PRACTICE** List two important facts about the pupil.

**READ THE PASSAGE** Think about the main idea of each paragraph.

## Deadly in the Water

Jellyfish can be beautiful to look at as they float gracefully in the sea. But most jellyfish have a painful sting, and one variety of jellyfish is considered the most dangerous living creature in the world. This creature, the sea wasp of Australia, can kill a large fish or even a human in minutes.

Sea wasps aren't the biggest jellyfish, but they can grow as large as a basketball. They have up to 60 long tentacles. The tentacles can dangle 15 feet (4.6 m) down into the water and are loaded with thousands of stinging cells. When the sea wasp's tentacles brush up against an animal, chemicals on the animal's skin trigger the release of the sea wasp's venom. The venom affects the nerves and heart of the prey. Usually the sea wasp uses its venom on fish, which it then eats. But sometimes humans are unlucky enough to come into contact with a sea wasp's tentacles. These victims can suffer excruciating pain, nausea, breathing problems, and occasionally even death.

Australians have developed an antivenom to treat the sea wasp's stings. Like the antivenom used for poisonous snake bites, it counteracts the poison from the sting. But there is an easier, although very unusual way to avoid stings in the first place. Australian lifeguards and surfers often wear women's pantyhose on their arms and legs! This thin layer of nylon prevents sea wasps from touching people's skin, which keeps the tentacles from releasing their venom.

**SKILL PRACTICE** Read the item. Write your response.

1. How do sea wasps attack their prey?

______________________________________________

______________________________________________

2. Why does the author include the definition of *antivenom* in the text?

______________________________________________

______________________________________________

3. What do Australian lifeguards do to protect themselves from the sea wasps?

______________________________________________

______________________________________________

**STRATEGY PRACTICE** In your own words, write a sentence that tells the main idea of each paragraph.

______________________________________________

______________________________________________

______________________________________________

**READ THE PASSAGE** Look for good details that help you picture events from the passage.

## Rain in Space?

One of the most thrilling and dangerous jobs of an astronaut is the spacewalk—leaving a spacecraft and floating in space while connected to the craft by a tether. One astronaut, Alexander Kaleri, took a spacewalk that was even more exciting and perilous than he had planned. On February 26, 2004, Kaleri and Commander Mike Foale were at the International Space Station in orbit around Earth. They planned to leave the space station to perform a list of repairs and experiments. It was the 52nd spacewalk at the space station.

At 4:17 PM, the hatch of the docking module opened, and the men began their spacewalk. The astronauts had five hours to complete their work.

Everything proceeded normally until 7:23 PM. At that time, Kaleri reported to Mission Control that there was water inside his spacesuit, saying, "I have rain inside the helmet. I have water inside the visor." He also reported that the water was "quite some amount, a significant amount. It felt like rain."

Immediately, officials on the ground grew worried. They found that a cooling device in the suit was not working correctly. They ordered the astronauts to return quickly to the space station, and by 8:12, the two men were back inside. It was the first spacesuit malfunction on a spacewalk—but it ended happily, with both astronauts safe and unhurt.

**SKILL PRACTICE** Read the item. Write your response.

1. What would be a better title for this text?

___

___

2. About how long did the February 26, 2004, spacewalk last? Explain how you know.

___

___

3. What went wrong with Kaleri's spacesuit?

___

___

**STRATEGY PRACTICE** Write details from the passage that were easy to visualize.

___

___

___

**READ THE PASSAGE** Pay attention to dates and important events described in the passage.

## Skeleton on the Ice

Zooming downhill on a sled can be incredibly thrilling. But what if you were going 80 mph (129 kph)? That's how fast the world's best competitors go in the sport of skeleton.

Skeleton competitors wear tight, stretchy uniforms that help lower wind resistance. They also wear helmets and goggles for protection. They need this special equipment for speed and safety while zipping down an icy track with hairpin turns.

Each skeleton sled holds one person. To take off, the athlete sprints as fast as possible, pushing the sled. Then the slider dives headfirst onto the sled, lying on his or her stomach. There is no steering or brakes on a skeleton. The slider steers the skeleton by shifting his or her body weight.

Skeleton began in 1892 in St. Moritz, Switzerland. Toboggans, which are long wooden sleds, were already popular, but the early skeleton sled was made mostly of metal. It looked like a skeleton, which may be how the sport got its name. The first skeleton race occurred in 1905. In 1928, when the Olympics were held in St. Moritz, skeleton became an Olympic sport. An American, Jennison Heaton, won the gold medal. The Olympics included skeleton again in 1948.

In 2000, the sport underwent another change when women began competing at the World Championships. The sport was part of the Olympics once again at the 2002 Games in Salt Lake City, Utah, when it became a permanent part of the winter Olympics. This dangerous sport with the spooky name is now practiced on a competitive level by men and women in 30 countries.

**SKILL PRACTICE** Read the item. Write your response.

1. How does an athlete start his or her skeleton run?

_______________________________________________

_______________________________________________

2. What happened to the sport of skeleton in 2002?

_______________________________________________

_______________________________________________

3. *The sport of skeleton was invented in 1905.* Prove this statement true or false using information from the text.

_______________________________________________

_______________________________________________

**STRATEGY PRACTICE** As you read, write down notes that tell you about the history of the sport of skeleton.

_______________________________________________

_______________________________________________

**READ THE PASSAGE** Pay attention to what happens in the passage and when it happens.

## The Greedy Tiger and the Big Wind

Long ago, the rains did not fall, and there was a terrible drought. It was hard to find food, and the animals became hungry and thirsty. Only one tree had fruit. It was a big, beautiful pear tree that grew in the middle of a field. Its roots reached deep into the earth, where they drank from an underground spring. Its pears were plump and juicy. The tree, however, was guarded by a cruel and greedy tiger. Although he couldn't possibly eat all the fruit that the tree provided, Tiger wouldn't let any of the other animals touch the pears.

The desperate animals went to Rabbit and asked for help. Rabbit helped them form a plan. Then he went to Tiger and said, "Tiger, a great wind is coming. It will be so strong that it will blow everyone off the earth!" While Rabbit talked to Tiger, the birds, which were hidden in the forest, began to flap their wings wildly, creating a strong breeze. Next, other animals beat on the ground and swung through the trees, causing the trees to sway and shake. Tiger believed that the great wind had come, and he was terrified.

"I will tie you down with rope so the wind cannot blow you away," Rabbit offered. Tiger agreed, and Rabbit tied him tightly to a tree. Finally, Rabbit called the other animals, who came out of the forest and ate every delicious pear on the tree, laughing at the selfish tiger who watched helplessly.

**SKILL PRACTICE** Read the item. Write your response.

1. Why do the other animals probably agree to participate in Rabbit's plan?

______________________________________________

______________________________________________

2. Why did it take all of the animals working together to trick Tiger?

______________________________________________

______________________________________________

3. What is the moral of this folk tale?

______________________________________________

______________________________________________

**STRATEGY PRACTICE** List the words or phrases from the passage that helped you visualize the details.

______________________________________________

______________________________________________

______________________________________________

**READ THE PASSAGE** Look for good details that support the main idea. Also, look at the order of important events mentioned in the passage.

## Dinosaur Buddies

Triceratops, the plant-eating dinosaur with three horns on its head, was long considered a solitary animal. Fossils for more than fifty adult triceratops have been found, and each triceratops was found with no other triceratops nearby.

Scientists revised their theory of the lone triceratops in 2005, though. In southeastern Montana, they discovered a site that contained triceratops fossils embedded in rocks that were 66 million years old. The person who found the site named it the Homer site, after Homer Simpson from the television show *The Simpsons,* because the plodding dinosaurs reminded the scientist of the cartoon character.

At the Homer site, paleontologists, or scientists who study fossils, found a group of three young triceratops fossils. It was evident to the paleontologists that the fossils were not found together by chance. The scientists deduced that the bodies of the juvenile dinosaurs had been deposited by a flood and that they were part of a herd of young triceratops that lived together.

Paleontologists admit they don't know how much time the young triceratops spent together, or even why they were in a group. The scientists believe the animals might have banded together for protection. The young of other similar dinosaurs have been proven to have lived in herds. Based on this finding, the scientists concluded that young triceratops probably lived in herds as well. They expect to find still more fossils of young triceratops at the Homer site.

**SKILL PRACTICE** Read the item. Write your response.

1. Why do paleontologists believe that young triceratops may have lived in herds?

2. How did paleontologists develop their original theory about triceratops? Cite text evidence in your response.

3. What killed the triceratops whose fossils were found in 2005?

**STRATEGY PRACTICE** Write two details that support paleontologists' theory about young triceratops.

**READ THE PASSAGE** Look for causes and effects that explain our ability to smell things.

## Get a Whiff of This

A fresh rose, a puddle of gasoline, or a trash bin of rotting garbage—you know it when you smell it! But where do smells come from? Odors are chemicals found in tiny molecules that float in the air. Anything with a smell, whether it is minty toothpaste or a moldy bathmat, sends off a mixture of these tiny molecules. When they reach your nose, you inhale and some of the chemicals reach nerve cells in your nasal cavity. Nerves send the message to your brain: "Something smells in here!"

Not everyone reacts to smells in the same way. Some people are very sensitive to specific smells, and others can hardly smell anything at all. Researchers have discovered that our ability to detect odors is genetic, which means that it is passed on from parents to their children. Every person recognizes smells differently.

Strong smells linger because the chemicals do not change easily. One of the most pungent aromas known is that of a skunk's spray. Getting rid of the smell on a person or dog that has been sprayed can be quite difficult. Some traditional methods, such as bathing in tomato juice, only mask the odor. Other mixtures, such as a mixture of hydrogen peroxide and baking soda, work better because they actually change the chemical composition of the odor molecules. But they can't neutralize the smell completely. Wetness can bring out a smell that you thought you had gotten rid of. So, a dog might smell OK when its fur has dried after a bath, but when it starts to rain, you might need to hold your nose again!

**SKILL PRACTICE** Read the item. Write your response.

1. What causes odors?

______________________________

______________________________

2. Why do different people react differently to the same odor?

______________________________

______________________________

3. What is the only way to actually neutralize an odor?

______________________________

______________________________

**STRATEGY PRACTICE** Explain which information in the passage is most important to understand for knowing how to deal with skunk spray.

______________________________

______________________________

**READ THE JOURNAL** Think about the causes for the effects you read about.

## Carole's Cooking Journal

***Monday, April 6***
*This month, we had to choose an optional activity to do during last period. Should it really be called "optional" if you have to do it? Unfortunately, I waited until the last minute to sign up. Many of the activities were already full, but I decided to join the Cooking Club because at least that way I would get a snack to eat.*

***Tuesday, April 7***
*Like many of my ideas, joining the Cooking Club made sense at first but is turning out to be a disaster. Most people have been in the club for more than a year, so they already know what they're doing. And since they all know each other, they aren't exactly interested in a newcomer.*

***Thursday, April 9***
*How was I supposed to know that if a recipe says to beat cookie batter, you're not supposed to do it with your fists? I thought the other kids would never stop laughing. And it's not easy to get cookie batter off your clothes.*

***Friday, April 10***
*More fun in Cooking Club. Now I know that chocolate mousse is a dessert and it isn't spelled m-o-o-s-e. "Mousse" and "moose" sound exactly the same. So I don't think my question about whether vegetarians can eat chocolate mousse was really that silly.*

***Monday, April 13***
*One of my bright ideas worked out for a change! Everyone laughed when I handed out the chocolate "moose" cookies that I made yesterday, but this time I was laughing, too. The peanut butter antlers were a huge hit. We're even planning to make another batch for the bake sale next week.*

**SKILL PRACTICE** Read the item. Write your response.

1. Why did Carole join the cooking group?

______________________________

______________________________

2. What idea did Carole have that proved to be a "hit" with the other members of the club?

______________________________

______________________________

3. Why did Carole beat the cookie batter with her fists?

______________________________

**STRATEGY PRACTICE** Write one question about Carole that you thought of while reading the journal.

______________________________

**READ THE PASSAGE** Look for evidence that supports the author's main ideas, or claims.

## How Identical Is Identical?

Everyone knows that identical twins look alike, right? Not quite. Although it may be very hard to tell identical twins apart, no two people are exactly the same—even identical twins.

Identical twins develop from the same fertilized egg, so they share the same genes. Genes contain the information that determines people's physical traits. While most people have their own unique set of genetic instructions, identical twins are unusual because they both have the same set. But researchers have discovered that those instructions do not tell the entire story. The environment in which each twin grows and develops also affects many aspects of their physical appearance and personality. Even small differences can have considerable effects.

Fingerprints are a good example. One might assume that identical twins have the same fingerprints. But detectives have known for many years that this is not the case. Like snowflakes, no two fingerprints are alike. Unique patterns on the tips of the fingers appear as the child develops in the womb. While genetic instructions are the primary influence on fingerprint patterns, researchers have discovered other factors that also have an impact. The rate of bone growth, or environmental factors such as pressure in the mother's womb and contact with fluid, can also affect the developing twins' fingerprint patterns. So even though two twins grow next to each other in the womb, they experience slightly different environments. As a result, they develop slightly different fingerprints.

**SKILL PRACTICE** Read the item. Write your response.

1. **Cite text evidence that proves that before identical twins are born, they can develop differences.**

2. **Name what identical twins share in common. Be specific.**

3. ***The amount of noise a fetus is subjected to can affect his or her fingerprints.* Prove this statement true or false.**

**STRATEGY PRACTICE** In paragraph 3, the author says that fingerprints are a "good example." What are they a good example of? Why?

**READ THE PASSAGE** Look for the reasons the author gives to prove the claims he makes.

## Mixing Ice Cream and Science

Erasto Mpemba took a cooking class at a high school in Tanzania in 1963. The class was making ice cream by boiling milk and sugar together and then freezing the mixture. Erasto put his mixture in the freezer right away; the other students waited until the mixture cooled. To his surprise, his hot ice cream froze faster than his classmates' cool mixtures! A teacher told him he must be confused. But then the teacher tried it and got the same result. Scientists call this strange phenomenon the Mpemba Effect.

In 2008, Olivia Mangino tried to demonstrate Erasto's result for a science fair at her school in New Zealand. However, she didn't have any details about what he had done. How much milk and sugar? What kind of pot? What size freezer? She had so many questions! She mixed the milk and sugar and poured it into two labeled bowls. She heated the Hot bowl in the microwave oven and left the Cool bowl as it was. She put both in the freezer and checked the temperature of each mixture every hour. Neither one froze. She tried again, using a different beater to mix the ingredients and a different freezer. This time, the cooler mixture froze, but the hot mixture did not. She concluded that many factors might affect freezing time.

Later, Olivia read about other people's experiments. In one, a metal container froze the mixture faster than a plastic container. In another, the hot mixture was still close to the boiling point and the cool mixture was close to the freezing point. Olivia's temperatures had been much closer together.

Scientists have proven that it is possible for water-based liquids to freeze faster when they start hotter. But they still don't know why. There are many factors that affect the result. They are probably having a delicious time trying to figure out the right combination!

**SKILL PRACTICE** Read the item. Write your response.

1. What evidence made the teacher believe Erasto's claim?

_______________________________________________

_______________________________________________

2. Why did the teacher probably have more success with the experiment than Olivia did?

_______________________________________________

_______________________________________________

3. What evidence led Olivia to her conclusion?

_______________________________________________

**STRATEGY PRACTICE** Write another question that Olivia might have wondered about as she set up her experiments.

_______________________________________________

_______________________________________________

**READ THE PASSAGE** Look for cause-and-effect relationships that the author describes. Think about the evidence that the author gives to support her claims.

## What Mosquitoes Like About You

Do you ever feel like mosquitoes single you out in a crowd? Do you think your blood must be extra tasty because you're the one who always gets bitten when no one else does? It turns out that mosquitoes do have preferences, but it isn't tasty blood that attracts them to their target. It's all about how easy a person is to find. Mosquito expert Susan Paskewitz explains that "the main things are how you smell and how warm you are."

Two scents that are particularly attractive to mosquitoes are carbon dioxide and lactic acid. Both of these chemicals are produced when you breathe or sweat. So, when you exercise, mosquitoes may zoom after you. That's because exercising causes your muscles to build up lactic acid. Also, your sweat emits carbon dioxide, and your body temperature increases. But not everyone produces carbon dioxide and lactic acid at the same rate. Some people produce higher levels, so they are more likely to attract mosquitoes.

Even your sense of style can affect whether or not you get bitten. Mosquitoes use color to decide where to land, and they prefer dark colors. Wearing a black or dark blue T-shirt is a good way to turn yourself into a giant target for mosquitoes. Wear white, and they might fly right by.

**SKILL PRACTICE** Read the item. Write your response.

1. Why are mosquitoes especially drawn to people who are exercising?

_______________________________________________

_______________________________________________

2. Why did the author quote Susan Paskewitz?

_______________________________________________

_______________________________________________

3. Name two things you can do to help prevent being bitten by mosquitoes.

_______________________________________________

_______________________________________________

**STRATEGY PRACTICE** What information does the author give as evidence of which senses mosquitoes use to find their prey?

_______________________________________________

_______________________________________________

**READ THE PASSAGE** Think about how the heroes are alike and different.

## Two New Superheroes Make Their Debut

Have you ever created your own superhero? I have! My superheroes are named Clockwork and Chrysalis. Like most comic book heroes, my superheroes fight for truth and justice. They deliver criminals to the police and have secret identities.

Clockwork spends his days as Henry Kadosh, a geeky, mild-mannered science teacher who frequently ruins his experiments in class. No one suspects he's really a brilliant scientist who has discovered how to travel through time. The youngest of eight children, Henry has always idolized his oldest brother Raul, also a scientific genius. After Raul was hurt in a lab accident, Henry helped his brother by taking over Raul's work. Eventually, Henry discovered the secret to making time travel possible. Now, as Clockwork, he serves humanity by traveling back in time and stopping crimes before they happen.

Chrysalis was born a Cherokee in 1833. She and her tribe lived off of the land and had a deep respect for nature. One day as she gathered food, she was simultaneously stung by a scorpion and bitten by a rattlesnake. The combination of the venoms gave her the ability to change into different animals and use their powers. For instance, she can temporarily blind enemies by becoming an octopus and shooting ink in their eyes. Or she can stun her enemies the way an electric eel does. She can also see as well as a hawk does. Chrysalis channels her power into fighting crimes against the environment. Once, after shape-shifting into an arctic clam to eavesdrop on whale hunters, she gained the clam's ability to live for centuries. Chrysalis has countless secret identities.

**SKILL PRACTICE** Read the item. Write your response.

1. How are Clockwork and Chrysalis like all other superheroes?

_______________________________________________

_______________________________________________

2. Describe the common thread in the events that led to Clockwork and Chrysalis becoming superheroes.

_______________________________________________

_______________________________________________

3. Do you consider Clockwork or Chrysalis more interesting? Defend your stance.

_______________________________________________

_______________________________________________

**STRATEGY PRACTICE** Describe a superhero you know about and how Clockwork or Chrysalis is like that character.

_______________________________________________

_______________________________________________

**READ THE PASSAGE** Think about how the different kinds of volcanoes form and erupt.

## Cinder Cones and Stratovolcanoes

What do you think of when you hear the word *volcano*? Most likely, you get a picture in your mind of a stratovolcano. Shaped like a cone with a crater at the top, stratovolcanoes are characterized by violent, explosive eruptions. Huge quantities of hot gases, ash, and rocks explode into the air. Lava rushes down the volcano's sides. These eruptions come from one or more vents, or "chimneys," inside the volcano. Stratovolcanoes are sometimes called composite volcanoes because they are built up, layer on layer, by repeated eruptions of ash and lava over hundreds of years. They can rise more than 8,000 feet (2,438 m) from their base. Some of the world's most spectacular mountains are actually stratovolcanoes.

Another kind of volcano is the cinder cone. Like stratovolcanoes, cinder cones are cone-shaped. They often have a crater at the top. Cinder cones, however, are tiny compared to stratovolcanoes. According to the U.S. Geological Survey, they are "built from particles and blobs of congealed lava ejected from a single vent." As the gas-charged lava shoots into the air, it breaks into small pieces. These small pieces quickly become solid and fall to the ground as cinders. As more cinders erupt from the vent, they fall on top of one another. Gradually, the cone-shaped mound of volcanic rocks grows taller. Once all the gases have escaped and eruptions cease, lava may continue to flow out of the vent and down the sides of the cone. Cinder cones usually build up over a period of several months to a few years. But they seldom grow to more than 1,000 feet (305 m) tall.

**SKILL PRACTICE** Read the item. Write your response.

1. Name two ways in which cinder cones and stratovolcanoes are similar.

_______________________________________________

_______________________________________________

2. Name two differences between cinder cones and stratovolcanoes.

_______________________________________________

_______________________________________________

3. You live near a cone-shaped extinct volcano that is 850 feet (259 m) tall. Explain which type of volcano it is and how you know.

_______________________________________________

_______________________________________________

**STRATEGY PRACTICE** Underline three ideas in the passage that you think are important to remember. Show a partner the ideas you underlined and explain why you chose them.

 

**READ THE PASSAGE** Use clues from the passage and your own experiences to make inferences as you read.

## Secrecy at Kartchner Caverns

On a cool November day in 1974, two young men made the discovery of a lifetime. Randy Tufts and Gary Tenen had been searching for caverns in the limestone mountains of southern Arizona. Limestone dissolves when water seeps through it, often forming underground cavities and deposits of a mineral called calcite. As a geology student and someone who liked to explore caves, Tufts hoped to find caverns in the area. But what they discovered was remarkable! What Tufts and Tenen had found was a "living" cave—a cave with calcite formations that are still growing—and it was untouched by humans.

Tufts and Tenen knew immediately that the caverns had to be protected. If word got out, curious visitors would come and disturb the cave. They would leave behind footprints and litter. The resulting microbes would begin destroying the delicate formations and ecosystem of the cave.

The two men shared their secret with just enough friends to limit the explorers' impact on the caverns' environment. For a year, they explored in their socks, touching as little as possible. The moist, humid cave was 2½ miles (4.0 km) long with two huge rooms and 26 smaller ones. Nearly all the rooms contained formations such as icicle-shaped stalactites, as well as more unusual deposits called soda straws, draperies, and cave bacon.

Eventually, Tufts and Tenen told others what they had found. First they notified the owners of the land, and then they told Arizona officials. A secret for just over two decades, the caverns became a state park. Rangers now protect the caves with elaborate procedures. Visitors enter through airtight chambers designed to keep dry air out of the caverns. Because of this and other precautions, geologists hope Kartchner Caverns will remain a living cave for many years.

**SKILL PRACTICE** Read the item. Write your response.

1. Why did Tufts and Tenen keep their discovery a secret for so long?

_______________________________________________

_______________________________________________

2. Cave bacon is comprised of which mineral? How do you know?

_______________________________________________

_______________________________________________

3. Why do you think these caverns became a state park?

_______________________________________________

**STRATEGY PRACTICE** Describe a place you know of that is worth protecting.

_______________________________________________

_______________________________________________

**READ THE PASSAGE** Use clues from the passage to infer information about the ancient library.

## Ashurbanipal's Library

Many of us have to pay fines when we return overdue library materials. Even worse, if we lose the materials, we may have to pay to replace them. While we may dislike these penalties, we should consider ourselves lucky. At least one early library threatened people with much harsher punishments.

The world's first known library with a system of organization and cataloged materials was in the ancient city of Nineveh, Assyria, near what is now Mosel, Iraq.

Unlike Egyptians, who wrote on a paper called papyrus, Assyrians wrote manuscripts on clay tablets. In the 1800s, archaeologists discovered vast numbers of these manuscripts in Nineveh's ruins. Scholars were able to read them and found notes at the bottom of each tablet that told who had owned them. They were part of the private library of King Ashurbanipal (AH-shoor-BAHN-ih-pahl), who ruled Assyria from 668 BC to 627 BC. Unlike many kings of that time, Ashurbanipal was able to read and write.

Scholars believe that Ashurbanipal's library contained more than 1,200 titles on thousands of tablets. Many had been taken from defeated enemies during wartime—a common practice at the time. Others had been copied from earlier tablets. The library contained dictionaries as well as tablets on religion, science, magic, and history. It also contained literature, such as the *Epic of Gilgamesh,* a famous story from the region. Materials were even organized into different rooms, much like today's libraries.

Although this was a private library, other people could use it. However, unlike today's library books, materials from Ashurbanipal's library contained curses threatening the wrath of the gods against anyone stealing or writing on the manuscripts. Maybe today's library fines really aren't so bad.

**SKILL PRACTICE** Read the item. Write your response.

1. Why does the author start and end the text by mentioning today's library fines?

_______________________________________________

_______________________________________________

2. Draw two conclusions about King Ashurbanipal.

_______________________________________________

_______________________________________________

3. Why did Assyrian manuscripts survive better than ancient Egyptian ones?

_______________________________________________

_______________________________________________

**STRATEGY PRACTICE** Describe something in the passage that you understood better after rereading it.

_______________________________________________

_______________________________________________

 

**READ THE PASSAGE** Use your background knowledge and information from the passage to compare Siara 5 to Earth and to make inferences about life in the future.

## Transfer to Siara 5

Aray Singer and his father gazed down on the fields of grain below as their sky taxi flew from the spaceport orbiting Siara 5, their new home. Many things on this planet were already familiar to Aray. Flying taxis, hearing implants that translated languages, and clothing that adjusted to the weather were common on Earth. Aray had been surprised, though, by how many activities were handled by machines on Siara 5. It seemed like the machines did everything. Unlike on Earth, visitors to Siara 5 transferred from spacecraft to sky taxi without the help of shuttle drivers or immigration officials.

As Aray looked more closely at the fields below him, he realized things weren't as automated as he had first thought. The land was clearly worked not by machine, but by hand—or rather, paw. Apes and monkeys were the workers that plowed fields, planted seedlings, and even harvested grain. As he and his father flew over orchards, Aray saw spider monkeys handpicking bizarre fruits, while orangutans packed the fruits into crates.

Aray and his father got out of the shuttle at a high-rise building and were greeted graciously by a staff member who offered to take them up to Mr. Singer's new office. The staff member was a gorilla! "Your meeting is already in progress," the gorilla said. Auto-translators made communication easy, even among different species.

Emerging from the elevator, Aray scanned the office: baboons, gorillas, chimpanzees, gibbons, and other kinds of apes and monkeys sat around a massive wooden table. "I hope you don't mind if my son sits in on the meeting," said Mr. Singer. "We haven't had time to go to our new apartment."

**SKILL PRACTICE** Read the item. Write your response.

1. How does the futuristic technology on Earth differ from our current technology?

_______________________________________________

2. How do you think Aray feels when he sees the apes and monkeys working on Siara 5?

_______________________________________________

_______________________________________________

3. What is the genre of this text, and when did you first identify it?

_______________________________________________

_______________________________________________

**STRATEGY PRACTICE** Describe how the passage is like another science fiction story or movie you know.

_______________________________________________

_______________________________________________

**READ THE PASSAGE** Pay attention to how each girl behaves and where the passage takes place.

## On the Outs

Shakira could feel the difference from the first minute she stepped into the classroom on Monday morning. Eva and Willa didn't smile at her, and the other kids didn't even look at her. "Why did I ever want to be Eva's friend?" she asked herself. Shakira hadn't even had that much fun being part of their group, although at the time she had thought popularity was more important than having fun. She had abandoned her old friends and her favorite activities, and now she had no one. After a while, though, Shakira had become invisible to Eva's group. Shakira should have known that they would discard her the way they had so many other people.

Shakira took her seat, her cheeks burning. "I didn't do anything wrong!" she told herself, but it didn't make her feel any better. Then she noticed Mattie, who sat to her right, motioning to her with a kind smile. Mattie and Shakira had been friends back in fourth grade, but Mattie had never gotten into Eva and Willa's group, and she didn't care. She just played her guitar, ran track, and did what she wanted to do without worrying about what anyone else thought.

"Do you want to sit with me at lunchtime?" Mattie whispered. Shakira nodded gratefully, knowing that she had never been invisible to Mattie.

**SKILL PRACTICE** Read the item. Write your response.

1. How is the setting important to the events in the text?

______________________________________________

______________________________________________

2. Describe how Shakira is feeling in the second paragraph.

______________________________________________

______________________________________________

3. How does Shakira feel about Mattie at the end of the story? Why?

______________________________________________

______________________________________________

**STRATEGY PRACTICE** As you read the passage, make notes about Shakira and Mattie to help you understand their character traits.

______________________________________________

______________________________________________

______________________________________________

**READ THE PASSAGE** Pay attention to what happens to Julius Caesar and when it happens.

## Beware the Ides of March

"Beware the ides of March!" According to ancient legend, that's just what a fortune teller told Julius Caesar, dictator of Rome, warning him to be careful on March 15. In 44 BCE, the Roman Republic was at the height of power. With his army, Caesar had conquered what is now Spain, Greece, Egypt, and France. He had brought social reform to Rome, improving the lives of average citizens.

Although Caesar refused to be called "king," he appointed himself dictator for life. Many Roman senators resented Caesar's great power, though. They wanted Rome to remain a republic governed by a group of senators, as it had been for hundreds of years.

More than 60 people plotted against Caesar, led by Marcus Junius Brutus. Brutus was Caesar's friend, but Brutus also wanted to restore the republic. On March 15, the ides of March, the plotters put their plan into motion and killed Julius Caesar.

The republic was not restored, though. Generations of emperors followed Caesar, ruling until Rome fell hundreds of years later.

**SKILL PRACTICE** Read the item. Write your response.

1. What did you conclude about Caesar when he appointed himself dictator?

______________________________

______________________________

2. When did the plotters' plan take place?

______________________________

______________________________

3. What was Brutus's motivation for helping to kill his friend?

______________________________

______________________________

**STRATEGY PRACTICE** Describe what you visualized happening as you read the first paragraph.

______________________________

______________________________

______________________________

**READ THE PASSAGE** Think about the author's view of the world.

## Trading Tusks

You may have seen elephants at a zoo and admired their long white tusks. But did you know that those ivory tusks are worth a lot of money? In the 1980s, the elephant population in Africa dwindled from 1.2 million to 600,000. Poachers, people who kill animals illegally, slaughtered more than half a million elephants just for their tusks.

Iain Douglas-Hamilton, a British authority on African elephants, brought this fact to the world's attention. Because of his efforts, the United Nations (UN) banned ivory trading in 1989. Poaching declined, and the elephant population rebounded. In 1993, Douglas-Hamilton founded an organization called Save the Elephants. It works to track and report on elephants, poaching, and ivory sales.

In 2002, the UN relaxed the ban on ivory trading. It allowed some countries to sell ivory that had been collected and stockpiled. These countries claimed that the ivory came from elephants that had died naturally. However, once the ban was eased, poachers once again began killing up to 20,000 elephants per year. Save the Elephants worked hard to inform organizations and governments of the effects of lifting the ban. The organization argued that the ivory trade should be outlawed again.

In June 2007, the UN once more approved a ban on international ivory trading. Douglas-Hamilton and Save the Elephants hope that the ban will help elephant populations increase to healthier levels.

**SKILL PRACTICE** Read the item. Write your response.

1. What is the theme of this text?

2. Use information from the text to explain what the verb *to poach* means.

3. Do you think the United Nations will remove its ivory ban again? Explain.

**STRATEGY PRACTICE** As you read, write notes about information in the passage that helped you understand the theme.

**READ THE PASSAGE** Look for value words that express the writer's views of animal adaptations.

## Lights in the Depths

Deep in the darkest reaches of the ocean, an anglerfish swims. A tentacle-like stalk extends from its head, and on the end of the stalk dangles a greenish-blue light, hanging like a lantern in front of the fish. The fish uses its glowing lure to attract a smaller fish. Snap! The smaller fish has become the anglerfish's dinner.

The remarkable bioluminescent light is created by chemicals produced in the anglerfish. It is a fascinating adaptation that helps the anglerfish survive in a difficult environment.

The anglerfish swims past a flashlight fish. This fish flashes its bioluminescent light to communicate with other flashlight fish. Then the anglerfish passes a squid, which rises to the surface, its glow helping it blend in with the moonlight. Swimming below the anglerfish is a loosejaw fish, which gives off a red light. Most fish can't see red light, so this helps the loosejaw find its prey without the prey being aware of the loosejaw's presence. But the anglerfish senses danger and swims quickly away from the loosejaw. As the anglerfish moves on, the light of an ostropod blinks behind it, trying to attract a mate. Like the neon signs on the streets of New York's Times Square, the ocean waters flash with bioluminescence. The deep-sea organisms are using their unique adaptations to survive in a variety of ways.

**SKILL PRACTICE** Read the item. Write your response.

1. What is the theme of this text?

2. What two words in the text indicate the author's opinion about bioluminescence?

3. How are flashlight fish and ostropods alike?

**STRATEGY PRACTICE** Describe how you visualized the anglerfish as it swims around the ocean depths.

**READ THE PASSAGE** Think about the lesson that Shawn and Neela learn.

## The Poster Contest

Shawn had been working on his entry for the school's poster contest for weeks. The topic of the contest was recycling, and the winner would receive the honor of having his or her poster displayed all around the school. Shawn was sure his was the best in the class—certainly better than Neela's! Shawn and Neela competed in everything, and their test scores and grades were just about equal. They almost never spoke to each other, but everyone in the class knew they were rivals. One thing Shawn excelled at, though, was art. His poster, which showed a garbage heap threatening to crush the school, looked really good. The only problem was the slogan, which was a little boring. It read, "Recycle."

Mr. Wu evaluated all the posters carefully and said, "These are all excellent, but there are two entries that really stand out." Shawn grinned as Mr. Wu held up his poster and the class clapped. But then Mr. Wu held up Neela's poster, too. The artwork wasn't great, Shawn saw, but the words written across the top were powerful. They read, "It's Your Planet—Recycle It!" Even Shawn had to admit it was a good slogan.

Then Shawn had an idea. "Mr. Wu," he proposed, "if Neela agrees, maybe we could work together. We could combine my art and Neela's words to make a really great poster."

Neela smiled at Shawn for the first time all year. "I think that sounds like a winning idea!" she said.

**SKILL PRACTICE** Read the item. Write your response.

1. What is the theme of this text?

_______________________________________________

_______________________________________________

2. Name two adjectives that describe Shawn.

_______________________________________________

_______________________________________________

3. Why does Neela agree to work with Shawn?

_______________________________________________

_______________________________________________

**STRATEGY PRACTICE** Explain how Shawn's words and actions reveal the passage's theme.

_______________________________________________

_______________________________________________

_______________________________________________

**READ THE PASSAGE** Think about why the author wrote the passage.

## Feeling Blue? Play Some Music

Everyone experiences bad moods now and then, some more than others. But help may be on the way. In recent studies, scientists have found that music can improve people's moods. One study conducted by the University of Maryland showed that listening to a type of classical music called *baroque* helped improve the moods of medical workers who study images of people's organs and bones. It also helped the medical workers feel greater satisfaction with their work.

But not only classical music helps people feel better. In fact, a Penn State University study of college students showed that any kind of music the students listened to helped produce more positive emotions, such as joy, affection, and calm.

How can you help *yourself* with music? Try a music-listening diary, as did the students in the Penn State study. Before you listen to music, record how you are feeling. Then get your cellphone, CD player, or radio and turn on your favorite kind of music. The college students most often listened to rock music, but you can choose any kind. Next, do whatever activity you would normally do while listening to music. For example, the college participants studied, exercised, and socialized. After listening to the music, write down how long you listened and how you feel now. Keep the diary for a couple of weeks, and find out if music really does make a difference.

**SKILL PRACTICE** Read the item. Write your response.

1. Why does the author describe the University of Maryland study?

________________________________________

________________________________________

2. Why does the author describe the Penn State study?

________________________________________

________________________________________

3. What is the author's purpose in the third paragraph?

________________________________________

________________________________________

**STRATEGY PRACTICE** Write a question you thought of before you read the passage. If you found the answer, write it, too.

________________________________________

________________________________________

**READ THE PASSAGE** Think about the author's purpose for writing the passage.

## Weather in the Prehistoric American Southwest

Today the American Southwest is a hot, dry place. In this region—which includes Nevada, Arizona, Utah, and parts of California—water is scarce. Yet fossils indicate that this was not always the case. Fossils of camelops (relatives of camels), American horses, and smilodons (commonly called saber-toothed tigers) have been found. Scientists believe these animals would not survive in the Southwest today. So how did they survive back then? Apparently, water was not as hard to find as it is today.

Scientists believe that more than one ice age has taken place on Earth. The most recent ice age ended about 10,000 years ago. Scientists call the period since then the Holocene period. During the Holocene period, animals had to try to adapt to a changing environment. Earlier, the Southwest had many forests and lakes, and temperatures were cooler. After the last ice age, however, many lakes dried up. New predators, including human beings, came to the Southwest, putting stress on the large animals that lived in the area. Because so many large mammals and plants became extinct during this period, scientists have named it the Holocene Extinction Event. Scientists have also detected further climate changes within the Holocene period. During the Middle Holocene period, for example, the Southwest was both warmer and wetter than it is today.

**SKILL PRACTICE** Read the item. Write your response.

1. Why does the author include facts about animals that used to live in the American Southwest?

______________________________

______________________________

2. Why does the author include information about the new predators that came into that area?

______________________________

______________________________

3. Why does the author include the last two sentences of the text?

______________________________

______________________________

**STRATEGY PRACTICE** Explain how using what you know about climate change helped you better understand the passage.

______________________________

______________________________

**READ THE PASSAGE** Use your background knowledge and clues from the passage to make predictions about what scientists will learn from King Tut's mummy.

## What Happened to King Tut?

A young Egyptian king dies when he is just 19, and he is buried in a hurry. His name is Tutankhamen, or Tut, and thousands of years later, an archaeologist discovers his tomb. The archaeological team begins to study everything in the tomb, including the king's mummy. The world is fascinated by the riches of Tut's tomb, but how the young king died remains a mystery.

In 1968, a group of scientists x-rayed the mummy and found what appears to be damage to the skull. "Could his death have been caused by a blow to the head?" they wondered. Theories started to emerge. Perhaps the king's young wife is responsible, or maybe someone envied the king's power.

In 2005, scientists examined Tut's mummy once again, using a CT scanner—a special kind of x-ray machine. After scanning the mummy, scientists determined that the archaeological team that originally discovered Tut had not been careful enough. They had dislodged some small bones when they removed Tut's gold mask. Now scientists believe that there was no blow to Tut's head, at least not while he was alive. Instead, they believe he died from an infection resulting from a broken bone in his left leg. It is also possible that he died from another disease. The mystery of Tut's death has not yet been solved, but murder is an unlikely explanation.

**SKILL PRACTICE** Read the item. Write your response.

1. Predict what will occur if scientists develop a new way to examine mummies.

___

___

2. The examination of Tut's mummy, which was done in 2005, was called a "virtual autopsy." Why?

___

___

3. Suppose that another Egyptian tomb containing a mummy is found. What do you predict will happen?

___

___

**STRATEGY PRACTICE** Write a question that can be answered by reading the passage. Have a partner answer it.

___

___

**READ THE PASSAGE** Think about what will happen next by using clues from the text.

## Bee Prepared

When the day of the district-wide spelling competition came, Juanita was nervous. She'd been studying lists of difficult words for weeks, but she was still afraid she'd get a word that she couldn't spell. Imelda, on the other hand, was confident. She had always been a good speller. In fact, she'd won her class spelling bee every year since second grade.

Juanita ate little at breakfast. She took a last look at a list of English words that come from other languages, and then she left for school. Imelda greeted her on the bus, and the two friends discussed their chances. "I'm positive you'll do well," said Juanita.

"So am I," laughed Imelda, quickly adding, "and I'm sure you'll do well, too."

That afternoon, Imelda and Juanita sat next to one another as the spelling bee took place. One by one, the other students were given a word to spell, and one by one they were eliminated. Finally, only Juanita and Imelda remained. The judge of the competition looked at Imelda and said the word *bourgeoisie.* Imelda looked startled. First she asked for the word to be used in a sentence. Then she asked for the word's origin. After the judge said that the word came from the French language, Imelda gave her answer: "That's B-U-R-J-O-I-S-E-E," she said.

"Incorrect," said the judge. Crestfallen, Imelda sat down.

"Juanita," said the judge, "if you spell the word correctly, you will win this round of the spelling bee."

Juanita repeated the word and then slowly began to spell it.

**SKILL PRACTICE** Read the item. Write your response.

1. What do you think will happen next? Why?

______________________________________________

______________________________________________

2. How do you think Imelda feels at the end of the story?

______________________________________________

______________________________________________

3. Predict what each of the girls will do after the competition.

______________________________________________

______________________________________________

**STRATEGY PRACTICE** What experiences of your own did the passage remind you of?

______________________________________________

______________________________________________

**READ THE PASSAGE** Think about the author's purpose, and use clues from the passage to help you predict how people might feel about Cleopatra in the future.

## The Legends of Cleopatra

There are numerous legends about Cleopatra, the woman who ruled Egypt during the time of the powerful Roman Empire. According to some stories, she was a great beauty. In others, she is described as hungry for power.

Figuring out what is fact and fiction about a ruler from thousands of years ago is difficult. However, we know this much: Cleopatra was part of a royal family, meaning she inherited her power. And she was romantically involved with two of Rome's most famous leaders, first Julius Caesar and then Mark Antony. Her relationships with both men influenced politics between the Roman and Egyptian Empires.

Another reason it is hard to find trustworthy information about Cleopatra is that, apparently, Romans were angry about her involvement with Julius Caesar and Mark Antony. After the men's deaths, Roman historians wrote accounts that portrayed Cleopatra as extravagant and selfish. Later, writers and artists used these histories as sources for their fictional accounts of Cleopatra.

Modern eyes may not find Cleopatra's profile on ancient coins so beautiful. Yet the legends about the entrancing beauty continue to endure.

**SKILL PRACTICE** Read the item. Write your response.

1. What is the author's purpose for writing this text?

______________________________

______________________________

2. Why does the author include information about the Romans' anger toward Cleopatra?

______________________________

______________________________

3. Suppose that new scrolls about Cleopatra are discovered in a cave. How would that affect what people think of her?

______________________________

______________________________

**STRATEGY PRACTICE** Write the most helpful question you thought of while reading the passage. If you found the answer, write it, too.

______________________________

______________________________

**READ THE ALMANAC** Study each section of the almanac page carefully.

# The World's Longest Rivers

| River | Length | Location |
|---|---|---|
| Nile | 4,132 miles (6,650 km) | Africa |
| Amazon | 4,000 miles (6,400 km) | South America |
| Chang Jiang (Yangtze) | 3,915 miles (6,300 km) | China |
| Mississippi-Missouri-Red Rock | 3,902 miles (6,275 km) | United States |
| Ob | 3,364 miles (5,410 km) | Russia |

### Fast Facts

- The Nile River passes through 9 countries: Burundi, Democratic Republic of Congo, Egypt, Ethiopia, Kenya, Rwanda, Sudan, Tanzania, and Uganda.
- The Amazon is second in length but first in amount of water carried and area of land drained.
- The Missouri and Red Rock Rivers are considered tributaries of the Mississippi.
- The Mississippi river system goes through only one country: the United States.

### River Terms

**Drainage Basin:** the area of land from which a river system collects water
**Hydrology:** the scientific study of water on Earth and in the atmosphere
**Main Stem:** the principal channel of a drainage basin, sometimes called a *parent river*
**River System:** the connected streams and channels that carry water from a region
**Tributary:** a stream or river that flows into a main stem

**SKILL PRACTICE** Read the item. Write your response.

1. How are the rivers organized in the chart?

______________________________________________

______________________________________________

2. Explain why three rivers are grouped together in the chart.

______________________________________________

3. Which river has the largest drainage basin? How can you tell?

______________________________________________

**STRATEGY PRACTICE** Describe a situation when the information from the "Fast Facts" section would be important or useful.

______________________________________________

______________________________________________

**READ THE TABLE OF CONTENTS** Study the content and organization of this book about weather.

## The Wild World of Extreme Weather

Table of Contents

**SKILL PRACTICE** Read the item. Write your response.

1. Where would you look to find the definition of a *microburst*?

___

___

2. Where might you find a chart that shows the length of the worst drought for each nation? Explain.

___

___

3. In which chapter would you look to find information about tornado hunters? Why?

___

___

**STRATEGY PRACTICE** Explain what the topics in Part Three have in common.

___

___

**READ THE DIAGRAM** Study the illustrations and the captions to help you visualize tectonic movement.

## Tectonic Plates

Earth's surface is shaped by the movement of tectonic plates that move into, against, or away from one another. Scientists study what happens to Earth's crust at the boundaries of these plates. There are three types of boundaries: **divergent** boundaries, **transform** boundaries, and **convergent** boundaries.

When the plates move, they cause earthquakes. The strongest earthquakes occur at convergent boundaries, while the weakest earthquakes occur at divergent boundaries. Earthquakes at transform boundaries are usually stronger than those at divergent boundaries, but weaker than those at convergent boundaries.

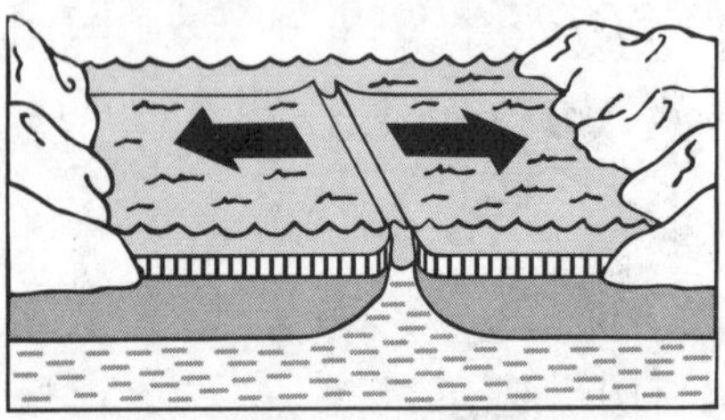

**divergent boundary**

**transform boundary**

**convergent boundary**

**SKILL PRACTICE** Read the item. Write your response.

1. How do the illustrations support the text?

______________________________

______________________________

2. In which direction do convergent boundaries move?

______________________________

______________________________

3. List the strength of earthquakes based on their types of boundaries in order from strongest to weakest.

______________________________

______________________________

**STRATEGY PRACTICE** What visual information from the illustrations was most important in helping you understand how the boundaries are different?

______________________________

______________________________

**READ THE AD** Study the ad and pay attention to how the information is arranged.

The **SOWAT BROTHERS** are back in town!

**Last year's shows sold out in SIX MINUTES! Don't miss this year's Comet Comeback tour.**

**RICK, MATT, and EBENEZER** sing all your favorite hits:

Close But Nowhere Near
Remind Me Why You Love Me ★ Love Shakedown
★ Don't Devour My Heart

*Special Opening Act:*

**FLUFFY PUPPY**

singing their new single
"Close the Book on Love"

**Just 3 shows!**
**June 3, 4, and 6**
**Center City Arena**
**8:00 PM**

Tickets available exclusively by phone through TicketBox
1-866-555-8269

SAVE THE DATE

The **SOWAT BROTHERS** with special guest **FLUFFY PUPPY**
NO REFUNDS

**June 6**
**8:00 PM**
**Sec 3, Row C, Seat 52**

**SKILL PRACTICE** Read the item. Write your response.

1. What line in the ad urges the reader to act right away? Use quotation marks in your response.

2. What is the name of the act that performs just before the Sowat Brothers?

3. What pieces of information are missing from this ad?

**STRATEGY PRACTICE** Identify an important piece of information that is shown on the ticket but nowhere else in the ad.

**READ THE INSTRUCTIONS** Read the steps and study the figures to learn how to make a shoebox guitar.

## How to Build a Shoebox Guitar

Here's a simple way to build your own musical instrument.

**What You Need:** shoebox with lid, glue, 4 to 6 rubber bands, scissors

1. Draw an oval-shaped circle on the lid of the shoebox, as shown in **Figure A**. You may want to trace a jar lid or small plate. Cut out the circle.
2. Mark lines to divide the cut-out circle into thirds, as shown in **Figure B**. Fold on the lines.
3. Glue the center third of the folded circle next to the circular opening on the shoebox to create a support for the rubber-band strings. This will serve as a fret, which is the part on a regular guitar that raises the strings slightly above the neck. (See **Figure C**.)
4. Stretch the rubber bands across the hole and over the fret, as shown in **Figure C**. Use rubber bands of different thicknesses and lengths to create different notes. The tighter the band, the higher the pitch will be.

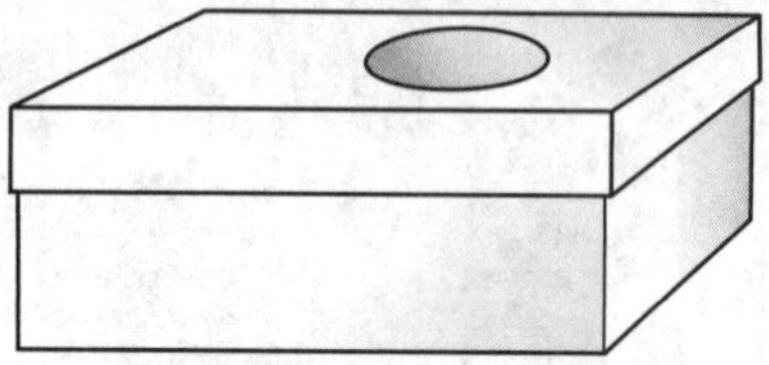

Figure A

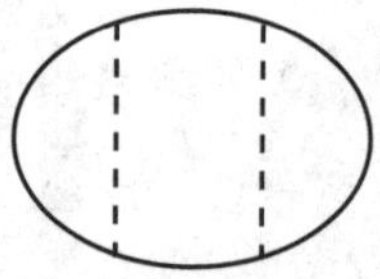

Figure B

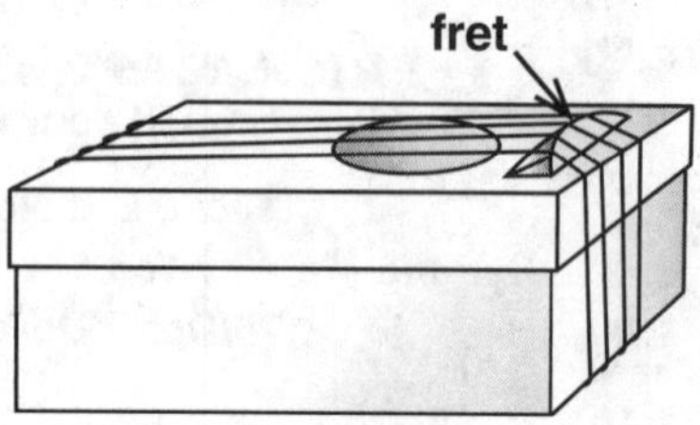


Figure C

**SKILL PRACTICE** Read the item. Write your response.

1. Based on Figure A, where should you cut the hole? Be specific.

2. Based on the instructions, what do the dashed lines in Figure B indicate?

3. What will happen if you put a tight rubber band around the instrument? How do you know?

**STRATEGY PRACTICE** Why do you think the author included figures with the instructions?

**READ THE PASSAGE** Pause after each paragraph and think about the main idea.

## Dog Smarts

All dog owners think their dog is the smartest. But researchers have determined the most intelligent dog breeds based on more objective measures—a dog's abilities to learn, solve problems, and obey commands. According to scientists, the 10 most intelligent breeds of dog obey a command 95 percent of the time and require fewer than five repetitions of a new command to learn it.

A dog's intelligence is not necessarily affected by what the dog is bred to do. The tenth-smartest dog is the Australian cattle dog, which, as its name suggests, is used to herd cattle. In ninth place is the Rottweiler, originally used in Germany to pull carts. Today, it makes an excellent guard dog. The golden retriever, fourth, is very popular around the world as a hunting dog and a companion.

The most intelligent breed of dog is the border collie, which excels at doing jobs and following commands. This dog, like the Australian cattle dog, was bred to herd sheep. Border collies must be able to listen closely and pay attention to their owners' commands. One border collie named Betsy understands more than 300 words. She is able to learn a new command as fast as a human toddler and is more intelligent than most of the great apes.

At the other end of the scale, the Afghan hound is considered the least intelligent dog. However, it's very likely that Afghan owners would disagree with this ranking.

**SKILL PRACTICE** Read the item. Write your response.

1. What is the first paragraph about?

______________________________________________

______________________________________________

2. Where is the main idea for the second paragraph stated? Use quotation marks to write the sentence.

______________________________________________

______________________________________________

3. List the four dog breeds mentioned in the text in order of intelligence, starting with the most intelligent.

______________________________________________

______________________________________________

**STRATEGY PRACTICE** In your own words, explain the main ideas of paragraphs 2 and 3.

______________________________________________

______________________________________________

______________________________________________

**READ THE PASSAGE** Look for important details that support each paragraph's main idea.

## Tulip-mania

For thousands of years, people have placed a high value on gold. But did you know that tulips were once valued just as highly as gold? Tulips came to Holland, a region that is now part of the Netherlands, in 1593 from Central Asia. At first, tulips were very rare and were grown only by wealthy people. This made the flowers a status symbol, and within ten years, tulip-mania had taken over Holland and spread to other regions and countries.

People sold tulip bulbs by weight, using the same measure as they did for gold. By 1624, a tulip bulb could cost as much as 3,000 guilders, or $1,500 in today's dollars. In months when tulips did not grow, traders would sign contracts to receive certain numbers of bulbs in the future, intending to sell them for still higher prices.

Tulips eventually became even more overpriced. Finally, in 1637, people realized that the flowers were not worth what they cost. The market for tulips crashed, and many tulip traders lost all their money. After that, the government set a maximum price that could be charged for a tulip bulb.

Today, the Dutch still love their tulips. The Netherlands produces three billion tulip bulbs each year, selling nearly one billion of them to the United States. The Netherlands is also the home of the world's largest flower garden, Keukenhof, where seven million tulips bloom each spring.

**SKILL PRACTICE** Read the item. Write your response.

1. Use quotation marks to write the main idea statement from the first paragraph.

2. Why did the Dutch government set a maximum price for tulip bulbs?

3. Cite text evidence that proves tulip bulbs were overvalued during the 1600s.

**STRATEGY PRACTICE** List words or phrases from the passage that were easy for you to visualize.

**READ THE PASSAGE** Pay attention to the number of steps involved in making maple syrup.

## The Sweetest Tree

If you like the taste of maple syrup, you're not the only one! And you're not the first. Maple syrup has been around since Native Americans discovered that the sap of maple trees could be boiled down to create a sweet golden or amber syrup. According to legend, the discovery was accidental. A Native American woman was boiling meat in a kettle that contained maple sap. The resulting dish was sweet and delicious.

Native Americans tapped, or cut into, maple trees to collect the sap. Then they filled hollowed-out logs with the sap and boiled it using heated stones. After a while, the sap became syrup, but the boiling was continued until at last the syrup turned into maple sugar. Native Americans used this sugar as their main sweetening agent and introduced early European settlers to it.

A lot of syrups sold today are made with corn syrup and are called maple flavored. This is because real maple syrup is more expensive. It is not unusual for a bottle of real maple syrup to cost three times as much as other syrups. Why is maple syrup more expensive? It is because the process that is used to make maple syrup today is difficult and takes a lot of time.

Today's process is not much different from what the Native Americans did. In early spring, maple trees are tapped and the sap flows out. Next, the sap runs into a tank and then to the sugaring house. There, the sap is boiled until it becomes syrup. Finally, the syrup is filtered. It takes 35 to 50 gallons (132.5 to 189.3 L) of sap from a maple tree to make just one gallon (3.8 L) of syrup. But most people think it's worth the time and effort!

**SKILL PRACTICE** Read the item. Write your response.

1. Describe each step that Native Americans took in order to process maple sugar.

_______________________________________________

_______________________________________________

2. Why is real maple syrup three times more expensive than maple-flavored syrup? Cite text evidence in your response.

_______________________________________________

_______________________________________________

3. In modern maple syrup production, what must occur after the sap is boiled into syrup for you to purchase it in a store?

_______________________________________________

_______________________________________________

**STRATEGY PRACTICE** In the passage, number the steps for making maple syrup today.

**READ THE PASSAGE** Read slowly and pay attention to the sequence of events.

## Explosion in the Night

On the night of March 22, 2009, in the small town of Willow, Alaska, Megan Warren lay in bed tossing and turning. She was worried about the report that she had to give in science class the following day. It was an oral presentation about the nearby volcano, Mount Redoubt, and Megan didn't like speaking in front of people. She knew her facts, though. Mt. Redoubt was an active stratovolcano. The last time it had erupted had been over a stretch of four months in 1989 and 1990, and the volcano observatory had issued a warning this past January that another eruption was likely soon. For the past week, lots of smoke and ash could be seen pouring from the top of the volcano. Scientists thought the volcano would begin spewing lava at any time.

Just after 10:30 that night, a huge explosion shook the house, and Megan awoke in a panic, wondering what had happened. Her mother rushed into her room and pointed out the window. Mt. Redoubt glowed red in the night. "The volcano has erupted!" her mother exclaimed. "Luckily, the ash is blowing away from us, so we don't need to evacuate."

Megan quickly dressed and went to the living room with her mother. Another explosion boomed through the sky, and Megan's father and brother joined them to watch out the big window.

"Wow!" Megan said, gazing at what looked like the world's most incredible fireworks display. "I'm going to have to change my report, but I'll bet my teacher gives me a few extra days to work on it!"

**SKILL PRACTICE** Read the item. Write your response.

1. **What happened to Megan just after 10:30 p.m. on March 22, 2009?**

__________________________________________

__________________________________________

2. **What did Megan do after her mother entered her room?**

__________________________________________

__________________________________________

3. **Prior to its 2009 eruption, approximately how much time had passed since Mt. Redoubt's last eruption?**

__________________________________________

__________________________________________

**STRATEGY PRACTICE** Describe how you visualized Mt. Redoubt as it erupted.

__________________________________________

__________________________________________

__________________________________________

**READ THE PASSAGE** Think about the main idea of each paragraph and the sequence of events described in the passage.

## The Flavor Gurus

Imagine what an amazing job it would be to develop and name ice-cream flavors! That's what the "flavor gurus" of Ben & Jerry's ice-cream company do for a living. While all ice-cream companies have people who develop flavors and name their products, Ben & Jerry's is known for its unique approach. The gurus explain that to create a flavor, they first decide on a concept. Then they find the right chunks, candy swirls, and flavors to add in. Next, they experiment mixing and blending, and finally they taste, taste, taste until they are satisfied with their creation.

There are several very creative flavor gurus, and each has helped to develop and name many of the more than 60 current ice-cream and frozen yogurt flavors. Some flavors are named after famous musicians, celebrities, or places. These include "Cherry Garcia" (named after musician Jerry Garcia), "Phish Food" (named after the band Phish), "Stephen Colbert's Americone Dream" (named after the television personality), "Jamaican Me Crazy," and "Dublin Mudslide."

There are many other great names and flavors. "Imagine Whirled Peace" blends caramel with toffee cookie pieces and fudge peace symbols. "S'Mores" consists of chocolate ice cream with fudge chunks, marshmallows, and graham crackers. "Turtle Soup" combines vanilla ice cream, cashews covered with fudge and caramel, and more caramel swirls.

Not all flavors are successful. Some have been sent to the "flavor graveyard," such as "Peanut Butter and Jelly," which failed with the public, and "Sugar Plum," which the company decided was just icky.

**SKILL PRACTICE** Read the item. Write your response.

1. Write the main idea of this text in your own words.

___

___

2. What is the first step in developing a new flavor?

___

___

3. What do the flavor gurus do right after they mix and blend?

___

___

**STRATEGY PRACTICE** List the most important details that helped you understand the job of a "flavor guru."

___

___

**READ THE PASSAGE** Look for causes and effects that explain why masks were used in ancient Greek theater.

## Masks in Ancient Greek Theater

In ancient Greece, plays attracted huge audiences—up to 20,000 people might attend a single performance. During the early development of Greek theater, one man had an idea to act out the poems and choruses that were previously performed by a choir. This man, Thespis, would act out all the characters in a play himself. He changed masks to indicate when he was playing a new character. Later, plays were performed by two or three men. These actors still used different masks to indicate which characters they were playing.

Masks served an additional purpose in Greek plays. Because theaters were so large, it was difficult for audience members to see changes in the actors' facial expressions. The masks had exaggerated features that were easier for audience members to see.

At one time, scholars believed that the masks also served as a kind of megaphone that helped the actors project their voices. However, today's scholars disagree with that theory because ancient Greek theaters were built with good acoustics. The sound quality was clear enough that actors would not have needed megaphones.

**SKILL PRACTICE** Read the item. Write your response.

1. Why did Thespis change masks throughout a performance?

________________________________________

________________________________________

2. Why was it difficult for the audience to see the actors' faces in ancient Greece?

________________________________________

________________________________________

3. Today, students who perform in high school plays are called thespians. Explain why, using information from the text.

________________________________________

________________________________________

**STRATEGY PRACTICE** Write two facts about ancient Greek masks, and explain how those facts helped the performers or the audience.

________________________________________

________________________________________

**READ THE PASSAGE** Think about what happens to each student and what causes these things to happen.

## Market Day

Theo, Laura, and Estefania were all excited for their school's Market Day, when sixth-grade students would get to sell their own handmade products to first- and second-graders.

Theo decided to make paper airplanes. He gathered a pile of used notebook paper from his desk and folded the paper to make ten planes. He tested each of them, and though they didn't fly far, he thought they were fun and creative. Laura decided to take orders for her drawings. She gathered drawing paper so that she could make the drawings once students told her what they wanted. Estefania decided that she would sell funny bookmarks. She got construction paper, scissors, and markers and created five different styles. After thinking about how many students would be coming, she decided she would make 20 of each style. A few hours later, Estefania had about 100 bookmarks ready for sale.

When Market Day arrived, the students set up their booths. Theo put all his airplanes on the table in two rows, while Laura placed her construction paper and pencils to the side. Estefania displayed one of each of her five different bookmark styles and stacked up the rest.

By the end of the afternoon, Theo had sold all of his planes, but he was disappointed because he could have sold many more if he had made more. Laura was unhappy that she did not make many sales. Because the younger students couldn't see examples of her work, they didn't know what to ask her to draw. Estefania, on the other hand, was very pleased. She had sold 95 bookmarks and knew she had planned well for the day.

**SKILL PRACTICE** Read the item. Write your response.

1. Why was Theo displeased at the end of Market Day?

_______________________________________________

_______________________________________________

2. What should Laura probably have done differently?

_______________________________________________

_______________________________________________

3. Did Estefania have a good Market Day? Explain.

_______________________________________________

_______________________________________________

**STRATEGY PRACTICE** What part of the passage prompted you to ask questions about what was happening?

_______________________________________________

_______________________________________________

**READ THE PASSAGE** Think about the claims the author makes and the evidence he gives to support them.

## Baseball Great Satchel Paige

Satchel Paige was probably one of baseball's greatest pitchers, although he had a limited opportunity to prove his skills. Paige was born in 1906 and spent the majority of his career playing for the Negro Leagues. During the 1930s and 1940s, when Paige was playing his best, Major League teams didn't allow African American players. As a result, African Americans had to play on all-black teams, in front of mostly black crowds.

In addition to playing for the Negro Leagues, Paige traveled around the country, pitching in small-town exhibition games against white Major and Minor League teams. Paige could throw a dazzling variety of pitches, and team owners were willing to pay him top dollar.

In 1947, Major League Baseball's color barrier was finally broken when Jackie Robinson became a first baseman for the Brooklyn Dodgers. Soon other black players entered the Major Leagues, and Paige himself was offered a contract in 1948 to play for the Cleveland Indians. By then he was 42 years old, and people joked that he was baseball's oldest rookie. Nonetheless, Paige's pitching helped the Indians win the division championship that year.

In 1971, Satchel Paige's contribution to baseball was officially recognized. He became the first Negro League player to be inducted into the National Baseball Hall of Fame, finally receiving the recognition he deserved.

**SKILL PRACTICE** Read the item. Write your response.

1. **How do you know that team owners valued Paige's pitching skills?**

2. **Why was Paige probably playing his best during the 1930s and 1940s?**

3. **Cite two pieces of text evidence that prove that Paige was a great baseball player.**

**STRATEGY PRACTICE** What information does the author give to support the claim that Satchel Paige was finally given the recognition he deserved?

**READ THE PASSAGE** Think about the claims the author makes and the evidence she gives to support them.

## Olmec Heads

Thousands of years ago, before the great civilizations of the Inca, the Maya, and the Aztec, another culture dominated Central and South America—the Olmec. These people, who thrived in Mesoamerica between 1200 BC and 400 BC, helped develop the calendar for which the Maya later became famous. Also, like the later civilizations, the Olmec believed in a corn god, and many other gods of nature. The Olmec also used innovative farming methods. But perhaps the most amazing accomplishment of the Olmec people was their art.

Explorers and archaeologists have discovered 17 gigantic heads that the Olmec sculpted from basalt, a volcanic rock found in the mountains. Some of these sculptures weigh several tons. The largest of the heads is over ten feet (3 m) tall. Each one has a different face and wears a helmet or a headdress. Some scholars estimate that it would have taken up to 1,500 workers and three to four months to move the heads.

For a while, scholars believed that because the heads had helmets, they represented Olmec ballplayers. The Olmec were known to play a game with a rubber ball that later Mesoamerican cultures also played. Now, however, archaeologists believe that the heads portrayed important Olmec rulers.

**SKILL PRACTICE** Read the item. Write your response.

1. Name two pieces of evidence from the text that prove the Olmec had links to later Mesoamerican cultures.

_______________________________________________

_______________________________________________

2. Name two pieces of evidence that the author includes to help readers understand the size of the Olmec heads.

_______________________________________________

_______________________________________________

3. *The Olmec lived in Central and South America more than 4,000 years ago.* Use text evidence to prove this statement true or false.

_______________________________________________

_______________________________________________

**STRATEGY PRACTICE** Write a question about information from the passage. Then have a partner answer it.

_______________________________________________

_______________________________________________

**READ THE PASSAGE** Pay attention to cause-and-effect relationships, and look for evidence the author uses to support her claims.

## Poison Ivy

Have you ever heard the saying "Leaves of three, let them be"? It's an old warning to stay away from poison ivy. This shrub or vine, which is found in much of North America, contains a sticky substance called urushiol oil. The oil is so strong that an amount the size of a pinhead is enough to cause an itchy rash on about 500 people!

If your skin comes into contact with poison ivy, the oil is very hard to wash off. In fact, once urushiol oil touches something, it can remain active for one to five years. A rash usually develops within a few days of exposure, causing severe discomfort and itching. Many people think the rash itself is contagious and can continue to spread. However, this is not the case. Once the oil has been absorbed into your skin, which usually occurs within 24 to 36 hours, it can't spread anywhere else. If new rashes do appear, most likely you have come into contact with poison ivy in multiple places, or the oil is on something you continue to touch, such as your clothing or your pet.

Instead of trying to treat poison ivy, your best strategy is to avoid it in the first place. The plant is characterized by clusters of three pointy leaves, with the middle leaf being the longest. Before you go camping or hiking, study pictures of poison ivy so you know exactly what it looks like. And whenever you are venturing into the woods, wear long pants instead of shorts, and trade in your sandals for shoes and socks.

**SKILL PRACTICE** Read the item. Write your response.

1. Name two pieces of text evidence that describe the strength of urushiol oil.

___

___

2. Why doesn't washing one's skin prevent a person from getting a rash from poison ivy?

___

___

3. Can a person get poison ivy more than once? Explain your response.

___

___

**STRATEGY PRACTICE** In the passage, what information about poison ivy is important for a person who is planning a hiking trip?

___

___

**READ THE PASSAGE** Look for similarities and differences between the ancient and modern Olympics.

## The Olympic Games

Today, people can turn on their televisions and watch the Olympics every two years, alternating between summer and winter games. The world's best athletes train hard, hoping to win a gold, silver, or bronze medal. However, the first Olympics was quite different from today's Olympic Games. Held in 776 BC at Olympia, in ancient Greece, the games honored the Greek god Zeus. The competition was a chance for athletes to bring honor to their city-states, just as today's athletes bring honor to their countries. However, in ancient Greece, only men could participate.

For 13 years, the ancient Olympics had just one event, a running race. Gradually, as with today's games, more events were added. The games expanded to include sports such as chariot and horse racing, boxing, and the pentathlon. The pentathlon itself consisted of five different events: running, wrestling, jumping, throwing a discus, and throwing a javelin. By comparison, today's pentathlon also includes running, but the other four events are fencing, pistol shooting, swimming, and horse jumping.

The ancient Greek Olympics ended around 395 BC and weren't played again for over 2,200 years. Finally, in 1894, a Frenchman named Pierre de Coubertin decided to bring the games back. The games were held in 1896 and included nine events: track, cycling, fencing, gymnastics, shooting, swimming, tennis, wrestling, and weight lifting. Today's Olympics include even more sports, such as soccer and skiing, and are now separated into the Summer and Winter Olympics. Cities around the world take turns hosting the Olympics.

For seven days before and seven days after the ancient Olympics, wars ceased so athletes could travel safely to the games. In a similar way, many believe that today's Olympic Games create goodwill, as nations exhibit strength through competitive sports rather than through battle.

**SKILL PRACTICE** Read the item. Write your response.

1. Name three ways in which the ancient Olympics differed from the modern Olympics.

2. Name three ways in which the ancient Olympics were similar to the modern Olympics.

3. What is the only common component of both the ancient and modern Olympic pentathlon?

**STRATEGY PRACTICE** Would you like to have attended the ancient Olympic Games? Why or why not?

**READ THE INTERVIEW** Think about how rugby and football are similar and different.

## *Youth Sports Online:* An Interview with Carlos Perreyra

**Youth Sports:** Carlos, you've played rugby for ten years. I hear it's a pretty brutal game. How does it differ from American football?

**Carlos:** First, rugby is much more active. In American football, each 15-minute quarter has only about three to four minutes of actual play. Rugby is almost the opposite. Each half lasts 45 minutes, and the clock stops only for injuries and player substitutions. Second, football players wear helmets and pads all over their bodies to protect themselves when they are hit or tackled. Tackles happen in rugby, too, but we don't wear pads. We play in shorts, long socks, metal cleats, and rugby jerseys. You have to be tough to play rugby! And since the clock never stops, a downed player has only one second to flip the ball to a teammate. If he's swarmed by players but doesn't fall down, the opposing team tries to rip the ball out of his hands!

**Youth Sports:** Are the two games the same in any way?

**Carlos:** Yes. Each game's objective is to get an oval-shaped ball across a line. In rugby it's called the "try line," and in football it's called the "goal line." In both games, you get a chance to score again after you cross the line. In football you can kick the ball through the goal posts or try to run or pass the ball across the goal line, but in rugby you only get to kick the ball.

**Youth Sports:** Do you think rugby is a better game?

**Carlos:** Absolutely! There's more speed and team play that you don't have in football. In rugby, the positions change. You don't have one person who plays just one position, and anyone can carry or kick the ball. A player can play offense and block for his or her teammate, receive a pass or recover a kick, or suddenly play defense if the other team gets the ball. It's very exciting!

**SKILL PRACTICE** Read the item. Write your response.

1. *In football, there is a single way to score points.* Use text evidence to prove this statement true or false.

_______________________________________________

_______________________________________________

2. Compare the timing in football and rugby.

_______________________________________________

3. Based on information from the text, are players more apt to be injured while playing rugby or football? Why?

_______________________________________________

**STRATEGY PRACTICE** How does the writer show who is speaking in the interview?

_______________________________________________

_______________________________________________

**READ THE PASSAGE** Use clues from the passage and your background knowledge to make inferences.

## Are Humans the Only Animals with Emotions?

Do animals besides humans have emotions, and if so, which ones? Scientists and animal lovers often debate this issue. In the past, many scientists believed that animals were not capable of showing complex human emotions such as empathy. Empathy is the understanding of and sharing in another's feelings. For example, if your little brother's turtle dies, you probably would feel bad for him.

Several recent experiments and observations support the theory that animals feel empathy. In 1964, one study showed that rhesus monkeys would not accept food if another monkey got an electric shock. Likewise, biologist Marc Bekoff reports that when he was watching elephants in Kenya, he noticed an elephant that had been crippled for years. Although the elephant moved very slowly, the herd never left it behind. They'd stop walking, check on her, and then wait for her. Bekoff also tells of Alaskan bear cubs that were orphaned when their mother was shot. One cub had been wounded, so he limped along and swam painfully slowly, but his sister never left his side. She even fished salmon out of the river for him.

There are reports of animals showing emotions besides empathy, too. In 2005, a humpback whale became tangled in fishing lines off California's coast. After divers freed the whale, it played with and nuzzled each diver, seeming to show gratitude. Gorillas, llamas, and many other animals appear to express grief when a mate dies. And then there's the story of the two abandoned terriers that were taken to an animal shelter. When one of them went blind, the other led his companion around the new environment by the scruff of the neck until the blind dog learned its way around. Maybe humans and animals aren't so different after all.

**SKILL PRACTICE** Read the item. Write your response.

1. Does the author think that animals have emotions? Explain.

________________________________________

________________________________________

2. What behaviors do you think animals use to display grief when a mate dies?

________________________________________

________________________________________

3. Briefly describe a time when you showed empathy.

________________________________________

________________________________________

**STRATEGY PRACTICE** Describe an example you have seen of an animal appearing to express an emotion.

________________________________________

________________________________________

**READ THE BROCHURE** Make inferences about ancient Cahokia by looking for clues in the text.

## VISIT CAHOKIA MOUNDS STATE HISTORIC SITE

### About Cahokia Mounds

Covering five square miles along the Mississippi River, the ancient port city of Cahokia was once home to at least 15,000 people. At its peak between AD 1050 and 1200, Cahokia had canals, fisheries, and irrigation for crops. In 1250, Cahokia was larger than the city of London. Rows of houses were built around plazas. Ceremonial buildings sat on huge earthen mounds. The tallest mound took 15 million baskets of earth and 300 years to build. Citizens traded in copper, elk, shark's teeth, and shells.

By 1400, the city was abandoned. Nobody knows why. Many things might have led to its downfall, including climate change, war, disease, and overuse of natural resources. Some people believe that cutting down trees and diverting natural creeks caused widespread flooding and crop destruction. These events, in turn, might have led to fighting and unrest in the community.

### The Name "Cahokia"

Because no one knows what the people of Cahokia called themselves, the site is named for a subtribe of the Illiniwek Native Americans who inhabited the area in the 1600s.

### Plan Your Visit

Cahokia Mounds State Historic Site is located in Collinsville, Illinois. Admission is free. A visitors' center offers exhibits, educational programs, and a museum shop. Self-guided and ranger-guided tours are available. Dress comfortably and bring sunscreen, bug spray, and water.

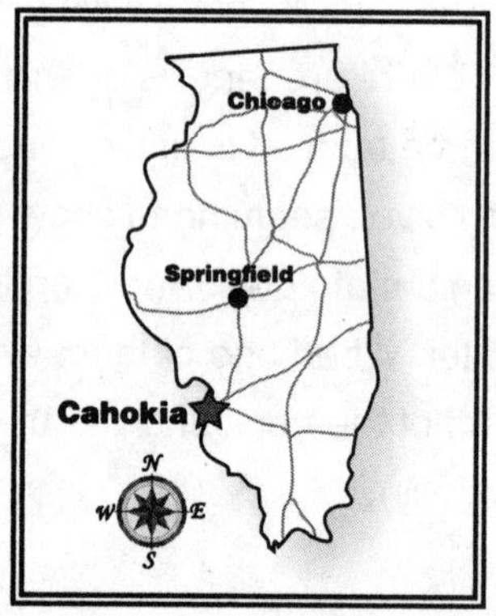


**SKILL PRACTICE** Read the item. Write your response.

1. Describe Cahokia in AD 1250.

______________________________________________

______________________________________________

2. What did Cahokian citizens use in place of money?

______________________________________________

______________________________________________

3. What do you think was the purpose of the earthen mounds?

______________________________________________

**STRATEGY PRACTICE** How is information organized in the brochure? Explain.

______________________________________________

______________________________________________

**READ THE PASSAGE** Look for information that helps you compare and contrast and make inferences.

## Effie's Visit to Egypt

Effie was an archaeology student studying ancient Egypt. She had been examining stone statues in Cairo's Egyptian Museum when *it* happened. Maybe the lunch she had wolfed down at the roadside stand had been bad. Maybe she hadn't drunk enough water. Whatever it was, Effie became dizzy. The last thing she remembered was slumping down onto the cool stone floor.

"Iphigenia!" Someone was calling her name. No one had used her full name for years! Suddenly, an old woman appeared. "Iphigenia! Get up! Where have you been? You are required in the bathing room." Her commanding voice made Effie follow her at once.

As they hurried upstairs, Effie noticed several statues. *Where am I?* she wondered. The statues looked new—no cracks or missing parts like the other ones in the museum.

"The pharaoh's son needs you to pour water for his bath right now!" said the woman.

"He needs help turning on the water?" Effie asked, surprised and confused.

"Unless you'd rather work in the fields than be a house servant, I suggest you get started immediately," hissed the woman.

Servant? Pharaoh? Where was she? Or rather, *when*? Hurriedly, she entered a room full of beautifully carved stone walls with water buckets along one side. A 12-year-old boy waited impatiently, tapping his foot. Effie scanned the bowl of grayish yellow blocks of soap and an array of oils and perfumes in handmade bottles on a table.

"Amun!" Oddly, she knew the boy's name. "Let's make you presentable to your family and to the gods!"

**SKILL PRACTICE** Read the item. Write your response.

1. What is different for Effie after she awakens from her dizzy spell?

______________________________________________

______________________________________________

2. What helped Effie figure out what happened?

______________________________________________

______________________________________________

3. How are the bath products Amun used similar to what people use today?

______________________________________________

**STRATEGY PRACTICE** Explain how the passage is like another story you have read or seen in a movie.

______________________________________________

______________________________________________

**READ THE PASSAGE** Think about whom the passage is about and where the events take place.

## The Longest Plunge

Pedro Olivia is a Brazilian kayaker, but he is not like most other kayakers. He is an extreme kayaker, and he takes his small boat where few other paddlers dare to go. On March 4, 2009, Olivia set a world record by plunging over the 127-foot-high (39 m) Salto Belo waterfall in Brazil. That's a greater drop than the height of Niagara Falls in New York! The previous record for a plunge over a waterfall was 108 feet (33 m), set in British Columbia, Canada.

Just before his record-setting plunge, Olivia paddled to the edge of the quarter-mile-wide (0.4 km) waterfall. Then, as he fell, he flipped his kayak upside down and dropped at a speed of 70 miles per hour (113 kph) and landed headfirst in the water. How did he survive the fall? He had picked a spot in the falls where a huge volume of water fell a long distance into a very deep hole. The falling water mixes with air and creates a much softer place to land.

Olivia was underwater for about five seconds. When he came up—still in his kayak—he realized that he had surfaced behind the waterfall. He climbed out of the boat and found to his surprise that the rocks were covered with large snakes! Slipping and sliding, he climbed out from behind the waterfall and made it safely to shore, surviving one of the longest descents ever made in a kayak.

**SKILL PRACTICE** Read the item. Write your response.

1. Where did Olivia's record-breaking plunge take place? Be specific.

______________________________________________

______________________________________________

______________________________________________

2. Name two adjectives that describe Pedro Olivia. Explain your choices.

______________________________________________

______________________________________________

3. How do you know that Olivia carefully planned his plunge over the falls?

______________________________________________

______________________________________________

**STRATEGY PRACTICE** As you read, underline words or phrases in the passage that tell you more about the type of person Pedro Olivia is.

**READ THE PASSAGE** Think about how a boy growing up in Sparta was affected by his setting and the events in his life.

## Living Like a Spartan

If you were a boy growing up in the ancient Greek city-state of Sparta, your life would be very different from what it is today. Soon after birth, you would be raised at home by a strict nurse. When you turned seven, soldiers would take you away to live in barracks with other boys your age. There you would learn to be a soldier, at times going without food and marching barefoot. You would learn to fight and survive. Punishments were harsh and frequent, and you would receive few rewards. You would hear stories that encouraged bravery, strength, and loyalty to Sparta. From this point on, your life would be under the control of the city.

At the age of 12, you would be sent out into the wild to live on your own or with a few other boys. For a year, you would hunt and cook your own food, survive cold weather, and fight off wild animals. Then you would return to life in the barracks for another seven years. You would learn more about warfare as you participated in military training and competition.

At the age of 20, your physical and mental skills would be tested. If you passed, you would be a soldier and full citizen of Sparta. The soldiers of Sparta were the best in the ancient world. In fact, the Spartan army stood undefeated until the battle of Leuctra in 371 BC. Spartan training, which encouraged strength and simplicity and discouraged emotional attachments and luxury, created a class of soldiers that has never been equaled.

**SKILL PRACTICE** Read the item. Write your response.

1. Where did ten-year-old boys live in ancient Sparta? Why?

___

___

2. What was the purpose behind Spartan boys living in the wild for a year?

___

___

3. Name two character traits that were admired in males in ancient Sparta.

___

___

**STRATEGY PRACTICE** What did you visualize when you pictured the life of the boys of ancient Sparta?

___

___

**READ THE PASSAGE** Think about the lesson the author learned.

## Jesse's Journal

**August 12**

I'm so thankful we're all okay. I never imagined I'd have to go through something as terrifying as what happened yesterday. At first I thought we were about to have just a regular thunderstorm. The sky got dark and the wind picked up. Dad came in early from the fields on his tractor. Then my sister Julia said, "Look at the sky. Doesn't it look weird?"

We went to the window and saw strange, heavy clouds. The sky had an eerie yellowish tint. I heard the wind begin to roar and started to feel frightened. Mom told us to run to the storm cellar, but I wanted to go to my room to get some of my things first. Mom grabbed me and made me stay with everyone else. As we ran toward the storm cellar, I saw a long, thin cloud drop down from the sky and touch the ground. The noise grew louder, like a train rushing straight at us. My little brother Mark started to cry. I picked him up and carried him down the steps into the cellar.

We turned on the emergency lamps and huddled together. Above us, we heard horrible sounds of crashing and tearing that seemed to go on forever. All I could think about was losing my computer and cellphone. I knew Julia was worried about the clothes she had just bought, and Mark was thinking about his favorite toys.

When it finally grew quiet again, we came upstairs. The whole house was gone—just gone. The garage next to the house hadn't been touched, and the barn was fine. We all had the exact same reaction. Instead of crying about what we had lost, we hugged each other and cried because everyone was safe. We still had what mattered most—our family.

**SKILL PRACTICE** Read the item. Write your response.

1. What is the theme of this text?

_______________________________________________

_______________________________________________

2. What kinds of things are the children worried about during the storm?

_______________________________________________

_______________________________________________

3. Explain how the family members feel after they emerge from the storm cellar.

_______________________________________________

**STRATEGY PRACTICE** Tell a partner which parts of the passage helped you figure out the passage's theme.

**READ THE PASSAGE** Consider the views that the writer has about people who work hard and how she conveys a message through certain details.

## A Day in the Life of a Large-Animal Vet

Rexanne Struve is a large-animal veterinarian in Manning, Iowa. She went to school in Kansas, thinking she would be a regular vet, treating mostly cats and dogs. The first time she treated a cow, though, she knew she wanted to specialize in large animals.

Today, Dr. Struve provides veterinary services for about 300 farms. At first, people didn't trust her. Many felt that a woman could not handle the hard work of treating large animals. But Dr. Struve decided to show them that they were wrong, and she succeeded.

Dr. Struve's day often begins with a visit to several farms, where she checks on pregnant cows and cleans and trims horses' hooves. She may deliver a calf, do surgery on a sick bull, or look in on pigs at a pig farm to make sure they are eating well. On some days, she will see as many as 16 different species, including ostriches and llamas.

When she is done driving from farm to farm, Dr. Struve goes back to her office. There she sees smaller animals, including dogs, cats, ferrets, and hamsters. Her job is exhausting and potentially dangerous. Large animals can be very unpredictable—and heavy! Still, she loves her work and the challenges it provides.

**SKILL PRACTICE** Read the item. Write your response.

1. What is the theme of this text?

______________________________________________

______________________________________________

2. Why does Dr. Struve's job have more variety than most veterinarians?

______________________________________________

______________________________________________

3. Why is Dr. Struve's occupation potentially dangerous?

______________________________________________

______________________________________________

**STRATEGY PRACTICE** Write the words or phrases from the passage that created images that were easy for you to visualize.

______________________________________________

______________________________________________

**READ THE PASSAGE** Think about whom the story is about and where and when it takes place. Think about the lesson or message the author is conveying through the story.

## New Green

Ming was on his way to school one morning, when he stopped to look up at the cloudless blue sky beyond the Bubble. It was another beautiful day. Ming took a deep breath. The air smelled fresh and sweet. The scent truck must have just passed by, Ming thought.

Suddenly, Ming noticed something unusual. In a little patch of dirt in the empty lot near the store that sold clean water, a small green post stuck out of the ground. Ming walked over to it for a closer look. The post was about a foot (30 cm) tall, with four or five green flaps hanging off it.

Ming recalled the holo-video he had watched in history class a few weeks earlier. It was called *The End of Green*. The video explained that things called *plants* once grew on Earth. The video stated that plants had completely disappeared from the planet. No one knew why, but this had caused problems with the amount of oxygen and carbon dioxide in the air. Scientists had scrambled to create new technologies for cleaning the air and turning carbon dioxide into oxygen. All life on the planet had nearly perished! People had built the Bubble to provide an environment in which everything could survive. This had been a difficult time in human history.

One of the plants in the video was called a *tree*. It had looked just like this post, only thicker and taller. It also had a lot more flaps, which were called *leaves,* Ming recalled.

"It's a baby tree," Ming whispered, reaching out carefully to touch it. "This is a real, live tree!"

**SKILL PRACTICE** Read the item. Write your response.

1. When does the story take place? How can you tell?

________________________________________

________________________________________

2. What would Ming probably think if he could see the community in which you live?

________________________________________

________________________________________

3. What is this story's theme?

________________________________________

________________________________________

**STRATEGY PRACTICE** As you read, write notes that help you understand the character, setting, and theme of the story.

**READ THE NEWSCAST** Think about why the author wrote the newscast.

## Report from the Irish Coast

This is Sean O'Malley, traveling reporter for MyFeed Youth Radio from the island of Inishmore off the coast of Ireland. Right now I'm standing on the outer wall of Dún Aonghasa (DOON an-GUS) Fort. This stone fort is a popular sightseeing destination because experts believe it may have been built between 1400 and 600 BC.

Today, the innermost wall is exposed to the sea, which lies 300 feet (91 m) below. Experts believe the fortress was built with circular walls that stood at least 12 feet (4 m) tall in places. It was also once several hundred feet away from the sea. The force of the ocean may have eroded the coast along with the fort walls.

In addition to the stone walls, razor-sharp limestone pillars set upright and close together helped defend the fort. These pillars did an excellent job of deterring attackers. Even today, visitors have difficulty getting past them as they explore the ruins. The defensive pillars are not unique to Dún Aonghasa. They have been used for centuries on every continent.

Visitors traveling to Dún Aonghasa should be prepared. Although the view of the ocean is breathtaking, the weather is often windy and cold. People with small children and people who have trouble moving should use extra care when visiting this ancient site.

**SKILL PRACTICE** Read the item. Write your response.

1. Why does the reporter explain about defensive pillars?

______________________________

______________________________

2. Why does O'Malley use the phrase "experts believe"?

______________________________

______________________________

3. Why does the reporter include the information in the last paragraph?

______________________________

______________________________

**STRATEGY PRACTICE** Write a question you had before you read the newscast. If you found the answer, write it, too.

______________________________

______________________________

**READ THE ESSAY** Think about why the author chose to write the passage.

## My Brother's New Gig

One evening a couple of years ago, my older brother Chris was listening to the blues on the radio. He had found a weekly blues program he liked, and he had listened to it several times. I happened to be listening with him one night when they played a track by Albert Collins. Chris went nuts! He thought that the song was the greatest blues tune he had ever heard! He liked Collins's casual singing style, but it was his guitar playing that made the biggest impression. Chris decided then and there that he would learn to play the electric guitar like Albert Collins, "The Master of the Telecaster."

I figured Chris's obsession with blues guitar music would blow over quickly. Chris was not the kind to put a whole lot of effort into things. This guitar-playing inspiration turned out to be lasting, though. Chris saved his money and bought a guitar and an amplifier. He took weekly lessons and practiced every day, no matter what. He even listened to Albert Collins's recordings over and over to try to learn how to phrase the music, bend the notes, and create a sound just like his hero.

I was impressed with how dedicated Chris was to his new hobby. He had never played an instrument before, but he took to the guitar like a natural. I could tell he had good rhythm and timing. He got pretty good pretty fast, too. He didn't even complain about his sore fingers or how long it took to learn the scales and chords. When he tried to play the solo parts to a few songs, he stayed with it until he started to sound just like Collins.

Last week, Chris spotted a used Telecaster guitar at his favorite music store. I hope he buys it. Then he will feel even more like his musical hero, and he will probably practice even harder. It has been amazing to watch Chris work so hard at learning how to play the guitar. He has been a really good example for me.

**SKILL PRACTICE** Read the item. Write your response.

1. What is the author's purpose for writing this text?

______________________________

______________________________

2. Why did the author mention Chris's practicing of phrasing, bending notes, and creating a sound?

______________________________

______________________________

3. What does the author explain to the reader in the final paragraph?

______________________________

**STRATEGY PRACTICE** What information from the passage helps you best understand Chris's motivations?

______________________________

**READ THE PASSAGE** Use clues from the passage and your background knowledge to make predictions.

## Red Sky at Night

An old rhyme used for forecasting the weather says, "Red sky at night, sailor's delight. Red sky in the morning, sailors take warning." Does the saying have any basis in fact? It turns out that it does. A red sky at sunset tends to mean that there are clear skies to the west, where the sun sets. A red sky at sunrise tends to mean that the clear weather has already passed, so storms might be coming.

Forecasting the weather has been practiced for thousands of years. The Greeks sent out forecasts to sailors as long ago as the 5th century BC. They used signs in nature to predict the weather. Today, of course, meteorologists use complex instruments that can measure and analyze weather conditions around the world and deliver accurate forecasts further in advance. Pilots, farmers, and many other people rely on these forecasts. Fortunately, most of us can simply turn on the TV or look on the Internet to find out what kind of weather is coming.

Nature still provides the biggest clues to the weather, if you know what you're looking for. There are two basic principles used in weather forecasting: Weather generally moves from west to east, and low air pressure usually means rain or other precipitation. So pay attention to the signs. If rainbows form in the west at sunrise, the sun's rays are striking moisture. Smell the flowers—their scents are stronger in moist air. What are the ants doing? Are they moving to higher ground? This could mean a drop in air pressure. Are the birds flying low or high? Falling air pressure bothers birds' ears, so they fly low. And if the sky is red at sunset, you might plan a picnic for the next day!

**SKILL PRACTICE** Read the item. Write your response.

1. Based on the text, what does it indicate about the weather if birds are flying high in the sky?

___

___

2. Do you think that today's sailors pay attention to the rhyme in the first sentence? Defend your stance.

___

___

3. What does it mean if a rainbow forms in the east at sunset?

___

**STRATEGY PRACTICE** Write a question you think of while reading the passage. If you find the answer, write it, too.

___

___

**READ THE PASSAGE** Make connections with the characters and events in the passage to help you predict what will happen next.

## Tamale Pie

"Open the tomatoes and corn," said Rosa's mom, Mrs. Chavez. "I'll chop the onions."

"Good," said Rosa. "Onions make me cry."

"Grind the walnuts," Mrs. Chavez ordered.

"I'm not sure the other Girl Scouts are going to like our tamale pie," said Rosa as she put the nuts into the grinder.

"Don't be silly," said Mrs. Chavez. "It's Cinco de Mayo, and this is a delicious recipe."

"But most people expect the main dish to have meat," Rosa said, concerned.

"Nuts are healthier. Now, shred the cheese." Mrs. Chavez put milk and cornmeal into a pot.

Two hours later, just as Rosa placed the tamale pie on the table, her dog Chivo started barking. "Hush!" said Rosa, opening the door. "It's just my friends!"

Becca entered the kitchen. "Something smells great! I brought a bag of chips and some guacamole, but I don't know about the guacamole—it sort of turned brown."

Dede walked in, uncertain about her refried beans. Kari brought some cold quesadillas, Jenna brought slices of mango, and Cinder offered another bag of chips.

"The table's all set, and the tamale pie is ready," said Rosa. "Let's eat."

Steam and the smell of corn and tomatoes rose from the edges of the golden brown cornmeal. "Wow!" the girls said at the same time. "It smells delicious!"

"There's no meat in it," Rosa said nervously.

"Who cares?" said Cinder. "Will you teach us how to cook, Mrs. Chavez?"

**SKILL PRACTICE** Read the item. Write your response.

1. What do you think will happen next?

___

___

2. Do Rosa's feelings about the tamale pie change from the beginning to the end of the story? Explain.

___

3. Why does Cinder compliment Ms. Chavez?

___

**STRATEGY PRACTICE** Describe a time when something you did worked out better than you had expected.

___

___

**READ THE PASSAGE** Think about why the author wrote the passage, and use clues from the passage to predict what will happen next.

## Last but Not Least

Duc-Hwan wasn't thrilled about attending the swim team's end-of-season awards ceremony.

"I don't see why we have to be here, Dad," he whispered. "It's not like I'm receiving an award. I came in last every time I swam this season."

"Not true," said his dad. "You were awarded ribbons at the last two meets."

"I can't imagine joining the team next year," Duc-Hwan said as he picked at his sack lunch.

"Hey, Duc-Hwan!" It was Coach Andy. "Hurry up and finish eating. It's time for the awards."

"Yeah, Coach, okay," said Duc-Hwan, trying to sound as if he didn't care.

"You're part of the Dolphins Swim Team, and we're about to begin."

Duc-Hwan wandered toward the bleachers and sat down. He dutifully clapped every time a teammate got an award. The ceremony seemed endless. Duc-Hwan let his mind drift. Suddenly, his dad slapped Duc-Hwan's knee. "Coach just called your name."

Duc-Hwan looked around. Everyone was staring at him. "Are you going to come up here?" asked the coach. Duc-Hwan rose slowly and made his way to Coach Andy, who held a large trophy. "Duc-Hwan, this is the only award that is decided by a team vote. In my mind, it's the most important award. You showed resolve and commitment even when you came in last. You exhibited real determination, and I hope you'll join the team next year."

Duc-Hwan scanned the crowd. Everyone was standing and clapping. Duc-Hwan grinned.

**SKILL PRACTICE** Read the item. Write your response.

1. What is the author's purpose for telling this story?

______________________________________________

______________________________________________

2. What will Duc-Hwan most likely do next year? Why?

______________________________________________

______________________________________________

3. How is Duc-Hwan apt to treat newcomers to the swim team?

______________________________________________

**STRATEGY PRACTICE** Write one question you thought of while reading the passage. If you found the answer, write it, too.

______________________________________________

______________________________________________

**READ THE LIST** Think about the text features that help you understand the information in the list of recommended books.

## Find Out More About Abraham Lincoln

***Abraham Lincoln's World,* Expanded Edition**
Learn about Lincoln and the world in which he lived. Writer Genevieve Foster discusses what was happening around the world during Lincoln's life as a boy, young man, and adult. 1940; Beautiful Feet Books. (376 pages)

***The Assassination of Abraham Lincoln***
If you'd like to learn history while reading a comic book, pick up this graphic novel by writer Kay Olson and artist Otha Lohse. Images and words work together to tell the story of Lincoln's fateful trip to Ford's Theatre and the hunt for his murderer. 2005; Capstone Press. (32 pages)

***Lincoln: A Photobiography***
This Newbery award-winning biography includes more than 80 photographs and prints from Lincoln's life. Author Russell Freedman's powerful writing reflects his detailed research. The book includes many quotations from letters, newspaper accounts, and Lincoln's own documents. 1989; Houghton Mifflin Social Studies. (160 pages)

***Lincoln Shot: A President's Life Remembered***
This oversized volume is designed to look like a newspaper from 1866, exactly one year after Lincoln's assassination. As you flip through the giant yellow pages, you'll be amazed by how author Barry Denenberg and illustrator Christopher Bing make historical events seem as though they happened just yesterday. 2008; Feiwel & Friends. (40 pages)

**SKILL PRACTICE** Read the item. Write your response.

1. How are the books in the list organized?

_______________________________________________

_______________________________________________

2. Why did the author include the information in parentheses at the end of each book review?

_______________________________________________

_______________________________________________

3. Which book might tell about what was happening in France during Lincoln's administration? Explain your choice.

_______________________________________________

**STRATEGY PRACTICE** How would the book list help someone who wanted to write a report on Lincoln?

_______________________________________________

**READ THE RECIPE** Think about how the recipe is organized.

## Easy One-Pan Supper

1 pound hot Italian pork sausage*

1 pound small red potatoes

1 large onion

2 bell peppers (red, green, or yellow)

1 tablespoon olive oil

salt and pepper to taste

*Time needed: 40 to 45 minutes*
*Servings: 4*

1. Preheat the oven to 450°F (232.2°C).
2. Cut the sausage into pieces that are 1" (2.5 cm) thick. Cut the potatoes in half and cut the onion into 12 wedges. Remove the core and seeds from the peppers and slice each pepper into strips.
3. Combine the ingredients in a bowl, and add salt and pepper to taste. Then spoon the mixture into a metal baking pan.
4. Bake for 30 to 35 minutes, stirring once after 15 minutes. Use a fork to check the potatoes. If they are tender and the sausages are lightly browned, the dish is done.

**You can substitute chicken or turkey sausage to lower the fat in the recipe.*

**SKILL PRACTICE** Read the item. Write your response.

1. Why is there a list at the start of the recipe?

______________________________

______________________________

2. How does the numbered list help the reader?

______________________________

______________________________

3. Why is there information included in a footnote?

______________________________

**STRATEGY PRACTICE** Why do you think many recipes have the same organization as shown above?

______________________________

______________________________

**READ THE PASSAGE** Pay attention to the information given in the map and how it supports the information in the passage.

## Cold-Water Winner

At 40°F (4.4°C), water is so cold that most people would freeze. But champion swimmer Lynne Cox is not like most people. She became the first person to swim from the Bering Strait island of Little Diomede in Alaska to Big Diomede in Russia. Cox baffled scientists who didn't think the swim was possible.

### Cox's Advantages

Most people would freeze to death in such cold water, but Lynne Cox can tolerate cold water temperatures. She has trained her body to function in very cold conditions. Body structure also helps Cox stay warm. Compared to most people, Cox has a very even layer of fat. This fat layer acts as natural insulation.

### From Cold to Colder

After the Diomedes challenge, Cox headed south—way south! She wanted to be the first person to swim a mile in Antarctica. "The marine mammals in Antarctica all have body fat to stay warm," Cox said before the swim. "Their blubber is very dense, whereas mine will be more like a cotton sweater. But I'm not going to be in as long as they are." Her natural insulation helped her stay in for 25 minutes; long enough to swim 1.22 miles (2.0 km) where no human had ever swum before.

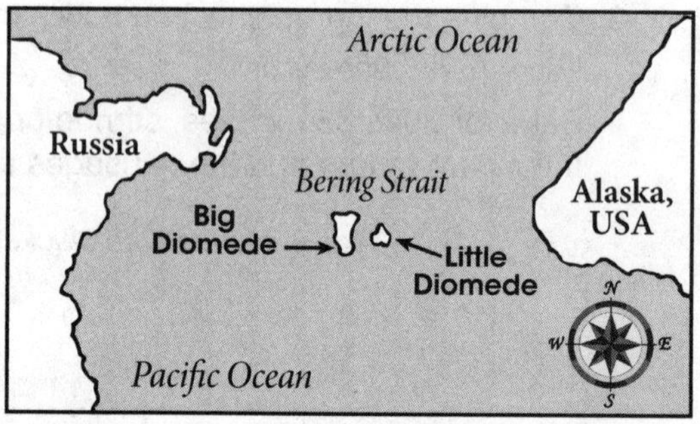


**SKILL PRACTICE** Read the item. Write your response.

1. Use the compass rose to determine the direction in which Cox swam in the Bering Strait.

2. Summarize the information given under the last heading.

3. *Cox's ability to swim in very cold water is based on three factors.* Use text evidence to prove this statement true or false.

**STRATEGY PRACTICE** If someone wanted to re-create Cox's swim in Antarctica, what information is *not* included in the passage that would be important to know?

**READ THE PASSAGE** Pay attention to the information in the graph.

## Voter Turnout

Every four years, on the first Tuesday in November, U.S. citizens vote to elect a president. Any citizen age 18 or over can vote. But not everyone exercises this right. For years, social scientists have studied voter turnout. Researchers not only count the number of people who actually vote in a presidential election but also figure out what percentage this number is of the total voting-age population. For example, in 2008, voter turnout was a record 131 million people. Although this was the highest number of people to vote in history at the time, it was not the highest percentage, because the population was so large. The graph below shows the percentage of the population that participated in each election since 1960.

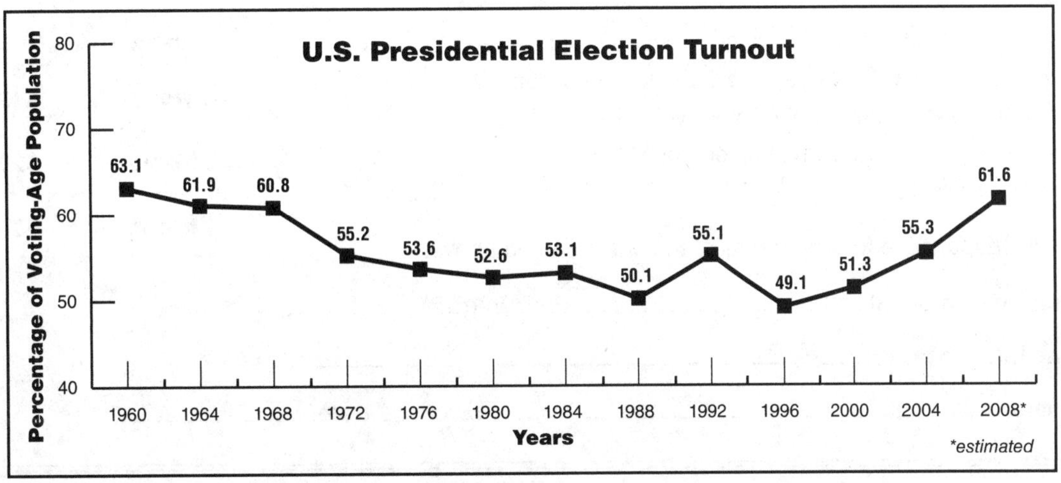


**SKILL PRACTICE** Read the item. Write your response.

1. Define *voter turnout* in your own words.

___

___

2. In which year(s) was voter turnout greater than 60 percent?

___

___

3. Why is there an asterisk after 2008 on the graph's x-axis?

___

**STRATEGY PRACTICE** Why is a graph better than a list for showing voter turnout over the years?

___

___

**READ THE CONTRACT** Pay attention to how the information is organized and the contract's different features.

# Wheel Have Fun!

### Contract for Bicycle Rental

By signing this contract, I, ______________________, agree that I will be the only rider using this bicycle and that I have the experience to use it safely. I agree to ride the bicycle no farther than 100 miles (161 km) from the **Wheel Have Fun!** office. I will return the bicycle by the time indicated below. For every hour the bicycle is late, I agree to pay an additional $10.

All bicycles include a pump, lock, and repair kit (patches, spare tube, tire levers). These items must be returned with the bicycle. There is no cost for using items in the kit, but please report their use to the rental agent at the time of return.

The rental rate includes insurance, which covers minor damage to the bicycle. This insurance does NOT cover any of the following costs:

- damage caused to property or other vehicles;
- medical costs related to an accident; or
- theft or loss of bicycle.

You are fully responsible for any and all of the costs named above.

| Rental | Rate |
|---|---|
| 1 hour | $12 |
| 2 hours | $20 |
| 4 hours | $35 |

**Period of Rental:** Start Time ____________ End Time ____________

**Name (please print):** ______________________

**Signature:** ______________________ **Date:** ____________

**SKILL PRACTICE** Read the item. Write your response.

1. What would it cost a couple to rent two bikes for 4 hours?

______________________

______________________

2. Name the two restrictions implied in the first paragraph of the rental agreement.

______________________

______________________

3. *A broken wheel spoke would be covered by the insurance in this contract.* Prove this statement true or false using text evidence.

______________________

**STRATEGY PRACTICE** What information in the contract is important for knowing what to do if you have a flat tire?

______________________

______________________

**READ THE PASSAGE** Think about the main idea of each paragraph.

## Atlantis: Myth or Reality?

Thousands of years ago, the Greek philosopher Plato wrote about a city called Atlantis, located somewhere near the Atlantic Ocean. The city he described was nearly perfect. The people were advanced in math, science, and engineering. The buildings and gardens were beautiful. Fountains flowed with hot and cold water, and stone walls were decorated with gold and silver. Plato told of Atlantis's end—how the city was destroyed in a terrible flood because its people did not properly worship the gods. Ever since, because the location of the city was never clear, people have wondered if Atlantis really existed. Many have searched for evidence around the world, even beneath the sea.

Some people believe Atlantis was once located on the Greek island of Santorini. The island was inhabited by the Minoans, a society with advanced scientific knowledge. Santorini was ripped apart by a volcanic eruption around 1500 BC, which could explain the lack of any remains of the city. Others think Atlantis was on Easter Island in the Pacific Ocean because Plato described enormous statues like the ones that have been found there. Still other people place the lost city in the mountains of Bolivia, in the China Sea, or in Africa. The fact is that no remains from Atlantis have ever been found. This has led many experts to conclude that Atlantis was made up, a perfect city that existed only in Plato's mind.

**SKILL PRACTICE** Read the item. Write your response.

1. What is the purpose of the first paragraph?

______________________________________________

______________________________________________

2. Why do many people believe that Atlantis came from Plato's imagination?

______________________________________________

______________________________________________

3. Did Plato blame Atlantis's destruction on a volcanic eruption? Explain.

______________________________________________

______________________________________________

**STRATEGY PRACTICE** As you read, take notes about the different theories people have had of where Atlantis may have existed.

______________________________________________

______________________________________________

______________________________________________

**READ THE PASSAGE** Think about what each paragraph is about and look for details that support the main ideas.

## Skywalking

Juan had always wanted to visit the Grand Canyon. He'd flown over it once in a plane, marveling at the way the canyon sliced through the desert landscape. Now he was on his way to the Grand Canyon Skywalk, a glass-floored bridge that jutted past the rim of the deep canyon. Juan's uncle, a Hualapai Indian from the reservation where the Skywalk was located, was one of the people who had helped build the bridge.

Juan bounced for 15 miles (24 km) over an unpaved road in his uncle's car. Finally they arrived at the Skywalk, where they received cloth booties to wear over their shoes. "We don't want anything to scratch the glass," Juan's uncle explained. "You can't bring keys or a camera on the Skywalk either, in case you drop them."

Juan and his uncle stepped onto the curved glass walkway. They were 4,000 feet (12,192 m) above the bottom of the canyon and 70 feet (21 m) out from the canyon's rim, seemingly suspended in the air.

"It's safe!" Juan's uncle assured him. "This walkway can hold 71 million pounds (32,205 metric tons) and withstand winds of up to 100 miles an hour (161 kph). The walkway is supported by a frame that goes 46 feet (14 m) deep into the rock of the canyon wall." Juan knew that it had taken amazing engineering skills to build the walkway. But to him, the truly amazing part was the view. He looked around with astonishment at the scenery—above, across the canyon, and far, far below. It was magnificent!

**SKILL PRACTICE** Read the item. Write your response.

1. Why does Juan's uncle know so many facts and figures about the Skywalk?

2. How are the Skywalk owners preventing scratches on its glass floor?

3. Would you like to go out on the Skywalk? Use facts from the text to explain your stance.

**STRATEGY PRACTICE** Describe how you pictured the Skywalk.

**READ THE PASSAGE** Pay attention to the major events in Cousteau's life and when they happen.

## The Man Who Loved the Sea

Jacques Cousteau was born in France in 1910. Although he was sickly as a child, he learned to swim at an early age and developed a love for the ocean. He joined the French navy in 1933, and it was there that he first used a pair of underwater goggles. Amazed at what he saw beneath the sea, he decided to build a device that would allow people to breathe underwater. In 1942, he finished the Aqua-Lung, a piece of early underwater breathing equipment that would eventually lead to the SCUBA diving gear used today.

After World War II, Cousteau began his life's work onboard the research ship *Calypso*. He worked with divers and scientists to photograph and gather samples of underwater plants and animals. In doing so, he learned about many ocean creatures that had never been studied before.

In 1960, he successfully worked to stop nuclear waste being dumped into the Mediterranean Sea. He worked tirelessly to improve the ecological conditions of the world's oceans and won many awards for his efforts. His television show, *The Undersea World of Jacques Cousteau,* ran from 1968 to 1976. The series helped raise awareness of the creatures who inhabit the world's oceans and their habitats. Cousteau died in 1997 at the age of 87 and is still celebrated today as one of the most important explorers and environmentalists of the twentieth century.

**SKILL PRACTICE** Read the item. Write your response.

1. What did Cousteau accomplish while he was in the French navy but before the end of World War II?

______________________________

______________________________

2. What man-made disaster did Cousteau stop in 1960?

______________________________

______________________________

3. How did the *Calypso* support Cousteau's television show?

______________________________

______________________________

**STRATEGY PRACTICE** Summarize the important events of Jacques Cousteau's life.

______________________________

______________________________

______________________________

**READ THE PASSAGE** Pay attention to the sequence of events described in the passage.

## The End of the World?

Asteroids—small bodies in space—have collided with Earth many times. The best-known strike occurred about 65 million years ago and created a huge crater in the Gulf of Mexico. After striking Earth, the asteroid likely caused huge tsunamis, or waves thousands of feet high. Dust particles probably filled the air. Scientists believe this dust blocked sunlight, eventually causing the planet to cool. Lack of sunlight may also have affected plant life, which is possibly what killed most dinosaurs.

A more recent large asteroid impact happened in 1908 in Siberia, Russia. As the asteroid exploded, it scorched and leveled trees for miles around. For several months afterward, astronomers reported increased dust in Earth's atmosphere.

Today, several scientists around the world track asteroid movement. When astronomers discover a new asteroid, they photograph it over several days. Then they use the pictures to create computer models of its possible orbits. Next, they compare those orbits to Earth's orbit. Based on the comparisons, they try to determine how close to Earth the asteroid might pass.

Scientists have created the Torino Scale to measure how likely it is that an asteroid will collide with Earth in the next 100 years. The scale goes from "0" (no probability) to "10" (definite impact). In 2004, astronomers observed an asteroid that they named 2004 MN4. They predicted it would pass near Earth in 2029 and gave it a rating of "4" on the Torino Scale. However, after studying it for several months, they decided that the asteroid will not strike Earth and changed its rating to "0."

**SKILL PRACTICE** Read the item. Write your response.

1. What happened during the months following the asteroid strike of 1908?

______________________________

______________________________

2. What is the first step that astronomers take when they discover a new asteroid?

______________________________

______________________________

3. Are scientists worried about asteroid 2004 MN4? Explain.

______________________________

______________________________

**STRATEGY PRACTICE** List the verbs and nouns in the passage that helped you visualize the passage.

______________________________

______________________________

**READ THE PASSAGE** Think about the main idea and details of each paragraph, and pay attention to the sequence of events described.

## The Life-Giving Parasite

Have you ever been swimming in a pond, stream, or lake and had a leech stick on you? You probably thought (or shouted) "Ick!" and tried to pry it off as fast as you could. But leeches aren't really disgusting, and sometimes they can save lives!

In ancient Egypt and later in medieval Europe, doctors put leeches on patients. They believed that the spineless wormlike creatures could cure all sorts of illnesses by sucking a patient's blood. In Europe and in the United States, millions of leeches were used throughout the 1800s. Doctors applied leeches to treat a variety of illnesses, from obesity to headaches. People soon learned that leeches could not cure most diseases and were not a good treatment for patients. However, in 1985, a Harvard University doctor changed people's thinking once again. He was trying to reattach a patient's ear, which had been cut off. He had trouble reconnecting the veins because the patient's blood kept clotting. He applied a leech to draw out the blood and saved the ear.

Since then, leeches have often been used in surgery where body parts are reattached. During surgery, a leech is placed on the area where the surgeon does not want blood to pool and clot. Then the leech secretes a substance that keeps the veins open and stops the blood from clotting. The leech sucks up excess blood, allowing fresh blood to flow, which helps the patient heal.

Some people are horrified at the thought of having a bloodsucking creature attached to them. But why not welcome a leech if it can save your life?

**SKILL PRACTICE** Read the item. Write your response.

1. When and why were leeches first used for medical purposes?

___

___

2. Write the main idea of the text in your own words.

___

___

3. Why did a doctor use a leech during surgery in 1985?

___

**STRATEGY PRACTICE** Write a sentence or two that tell how the use of leeches has changed over time.

___

___

**READ THE PASSAGE** Look for the effects of text messaging that the writer identifies.

## How Much Texting Is Too Much?

Cellphone calling plans that allow users to send unlimited text messages are popular. In 2015, an average American teen sent 3,000 text messages each month. That's about 100 messages a day, although many teens commonly send hundreds of messages per day. So, are there any downsides to texting?

The physical action of typing and sending so many text messages could injure your thumbs. When you perform the same action many times, you can get something called a repetitive stress injury, which causes painful muscle cramps. Doctors believe the damage is temporary and can heal if the action is stopped.

Sending and receiving text messages can also interfere with sleep. Ringtones or vibrations can break one's concentration.

Still, many people like texting because it helps them stay in touch with their family and friends. Texting is also a convenient way to communicate when you cannot talk on the phone. You can also send pictures through texts. Ultimately, people can decide how much texting is right for themselves.

**SKILL PRACTICE** Read the item. Write your response.

1. Can the repetitive stress injury caused by texting heal? Explain.

2. Cite text evidence that shows that texting is popular.

3. What is one positive result of texting?

**STRATEGY PRACTICE** Write one question you have about this text's topic.

**READ THE PASSAGE** Think about what happens in the passage and the reasons why those things happen.

## Which Button Do I Press?

My brother Micha's high school graduation was almost over, and I was still fumbling with my new digital camera. I had gotten it for my birthday, but I had never read the directions. That's why I spent most of the ceremony trying to figure out how to turn the camera on. And when I finally did, all I saw on the screen were a bunch of mysterious icons.

Soon the principal was calling students' names. Each graduate walked happily across the stage to get his or her diploma. It was almost Micha's turn! I started pressing buttons at random until the camera beeped. Had I taken a picture? There was no time to check because the principal called Micha's name. I peered through the camera's viewfinder.

Micha strode over to the principal, smiling ear to ear. Then, suddenly, he did the most amazing thing. He jumped into the air and did a complete flip! When he landed, the crowd went wild. I tried to snap a picture, but the camera just beeped again, like it was making fun of me.

After the ceremony, I handed the camera to Micha and apologized for being such a lousy photographer. "What are you talking about, Sasha?" he said excitedly. "You got the whole thing on video!"

I must have hit the button for video instead of photo. Micha ended up posting the clip on the Internet for our friends and family to see, and everyone keeps congratulating me on my fine camera work. Now, if only I could figure out which button I pressed.

**SKILL PRACTICE** Read the item. Write your response.

1. Why is Sasha fumbling with her camera at the start of the story?

_______________________________________________

_______________________________________________

2. Why does Micha do a flip?

_______________________________________________

_______________________________________________

3. What happens as a result of Sasha recording a video?

_______________________________________________

_______________________________________________

**STRATEGY PRACTICE** Write a question you asked yourself while reading. If you found the answer, write it, too.

_______________________________________________

_______________________________________________

**READ THE PASSAGE** Think about the author's claims and the evidence he gives to support those claims.

## Mystery Under the Sea

Basking sharks are the second-largest kind of shark in the world. In the summer, they are easy to spot. These huge, slow-moving North Atlantic fish eat plankton near the water's surface. But during the winter, basking sharks seem to disappear. Where do they go? Scientists have discovered the answer.

Experts used to think that the sharks hibernated in deeper ocean waters during the winter. However, a new study disproves that theory. Researchers tagged 25 basking sharks near Cape Cod, Massachusetts, and used satellites to track the sharks' movements. The tags also sent information about water depth, temperature, and light levels. The results showed that basking sharks migrate much farther than anyone expected. They don't hibernate deep in the ocean. Instead, they swim huge distances from the North Atlantic to warmer tropical water. One of the tagged sharks even swam 5,500 miles (8,851 km).

Information from the tags showed that during the winter, sharks swim much deeper than in the summer. When they migrate, they swim at depths up to 3,000 feet (914 m), and they stay at those depths for three or four months. That explains why basking sharks seem to disappear in the winter—they are too deep to be seen.

**SKILL PRACTICE** Read the item. Write your response.

1. What part of the scientists' original theory turned out to be correct?

_______________________________________________

_______________________________________________

2. What strategy did scientists use to find out where basking sharks go during the winter?

_______________________________________________

_______________________________________________

3. Why had no one ever seen the basking sharks in their winter territory?

_______________________________________________

_______________________________________________

**STRATEGY PRACTICE** Underline the information in the passage that helps you answer the three questions from the skill practice activity.

**READ THE PASSAGE** Think about the evidence that the author gives to support her claims.

## Dog Park Proposal

Our dogs need a place to play! It's time to create a dog park in Oakwood. Musket Field at the corner of Oak Street and Prospect Avenue is the perfect location for the new dog park.

Why do we need a dog park? People in Oakwood love dogs. There are dogs living in three out of every five homes in Oakwood. That's higher than the national average!

Why Musket Field? First of all, there are 21 public baseball fields in Oakwood. These fields are empty an average of 40 percent of the time from 8 AM to 8 PM. One less field will not hurt the baseball teams. Secondly, for years, Musket Field has been the least popular playing field in Oakwood, mainly because of how poorly it drains. In fact, most residents don't even know the field's real name. They only know it by the nickname "Mudpit Field." Converting the field to a dog park would include leveling the ground and laying down gravel, which would improve drainage and eliminate a community eyesore.

Where will the money come from? The Friends of Oakwood Dogs have already raised 30 percent of the predicted costs. A citizens' fundraising drive will generate another 25 percent of the funds. The remaining cost could come from the Oakwood Community Recreation Fund.

Please attend the community board meeting on March 14 and voice your support for the Oakwood Dog Park. Speak up for our dogs, because they can't speak for themselves!

**SKILL PRACTICE** Read the item. Write your response.

1. What is the author's purpose for writing this text?

______________________________________________

______________________________________________

2. Why does the author mention that Musket Field is an unpopular baseball field?

______________________________________________

______________________________________________

3. What support does the author offer regarding the claim that a dog park will beautify Musket Field?

______________________________________________

______________________________________________

**STRATEGY PRACTICE** Before you read the passage, write a question you have about the topic. If you find the answer as you read, write it, too.

______________________________________________

______________________________________________

**READ THE PASSAGE** Look for causes and effects in the passage, and look for evidence the author gives to support her claims.

## The Seeing Eye

In 1927, an American named Dorothy Harrison Eustis traveled to Switzerland to open a dog kennel. She was interested in breeding German shepherds for certain kinds of work. As part of her research, she visited a school where these dogs were being trained to help World War I veterans who had lost their sight. Eustis was so inspired by what she saw that she wrote an article about the school. It was published in *The Saturday Evening Post* on November 5, 1927.

Morris Frank, a blind man from Tennessee, was inspired by Eustis's article. He wrote her a letter asking if she would help him get a trained dog so that he could leave his home more easily and be more independent. Eustis agreed. Frank traveled to Switzerland to meet Eustis and work with a guide dog. When Frank and his new dog Buddy came back to Tennessee in 1928, reporters were astonished by the efficient working partnership between a person and a dog. Frank sent Eustis a telegram with just one word: "Success."

In 1929, Frank and Eustis helped start a dog-training school called The Seeing Eye. The school is now in New Jersey and still breeds and trains hundreds of dogs every year. People come from all over to meet their guide dogs and learn how to work together as effective teams. But not every dog is a perfect match for just any person. The trainers must carefully match dogs with people. A person needs to be strong to control the dog, and both the dog and the person should walk at the same natural pace. Other factors, such as personality and the type of home environment, are also used to help match people with their amazing animal companions.

**SKILL PRACTICE** Read the item. Write your response.

1. Why did Morris Frank write to Dorothy Eustis?

___

___

2. Draw an inference about the breed that was used for the original Seeing Eye dogs.

___

3. What may happen if a trainer matches a dog with the wrong person?

___

___

**STRATEGY PRACTICE** The author states that "not every dog is a perfect match for just any person." What information in the article supports this claim?

___

___

**READ THE PASSAGE** Look for the similarities and differences between Egyptian pyramids and the pyramids in Mexico.

## Comparing the World's Pyramids

Most people know about ancient Egyptian pyramids. Constructed of limestone blocks between 2630 and 2250 BC, these vast tombs were built to house Egypt's kings (called pharaohs) in the afterlife. The pyramids' great size and beauty also symbolized the pharaohs' power. The largest pyramid, at Giza, was 481 feet (147 m) high.

Ancient Egyptians believed that part of the pharaoh's spirit remained with the body, so the body had to be preserved as a mummy. In order for the pharaoh to rule in the afterlife, food and other items were buried in the pyramid with the pharaoh's mummy.

Like the Egyptians, Mesoamericans built pyramids, too. These pyramids were built from rubble covered with stucco. Mexico's tallest pyramid, the Templo Mayor in Mexico City, Mexico, is 217 feet (66 m) high.

Like Egypt's first pyramid, but unlike later Egyptian pyramids, the Mexican pyramids were step pyramids with flat tops. They were built as bases for temples and ceremonies, not as tombs. Priests climbed the steps and stood at the top to speak. The acoustics of El Castillo at Chichén Itzá in Mexico, built around AD 800, carried a speaker's voice perfectly from the top of the pyramid to the people below. Today, people still visit this and other remarkable pyramids.

**SKILL PRACTICE** Read the item. Write your response.

1. How are Egyptian and Mesoamerican pyramids alike?

______________________________

______________________________

2. Describe the difference in the appearance of an Egyptian and a Mesoamerican pyramid.

______________________________

______________________________

3. Compare the purpose of an Egyptian pyramid to the purpose of a Mesoamerican one.

______________________________

______________________________

**STRATEGY PRACTICE** Describe one other thing you know about either the ancient Egyptians or the Mesoamericans.

______________________________

______________________________

**READ THE PASSAGE** Think about the similarities and differences between fruits and vegetables.

## A Fruit? A Vegetable? Which Is It?

What's the difference between a fruit and a vegetable? The differences are not as straightforward as you may think. The way you categorize these foods may depend on whether you're a scientist or a chef. For example, most people think of fruits as sweet and vegetables as bitter, bland, or savory. So what would you call a tomato? Tomatoes are often added to foods such as pasta sauce, tacos, and stews, so most of us think of them as vegetables. However, a tomato is really a fruit. What about cucumbers and peas? They're green like many vegetables, and we eat them as side dishes, not on ice cream or cereal! But they're actually fruits, too. So are squash, beans, and nuts.

Botanists, or scientists who study plants, define a fruit as any plant part that can generate a new plant or the seeds of the parent plant. A fruit is formed from the flower of a plant.

Vegetables, on the other hand, are all the other edible parts of a plant—the roots, the stalks, the leaves, and so on. Carrots and beets and potatoes are root vegetables; celery and asparagus are stalks; and leafy vegetables include lettuce, kale, and spinach.

Of course, when we're eating, we don't worry so much about whether our food is a fruit or a vegetable. We mainly focus on flavor. But the debate over fruits and vegetables can get heated. In a famous court case (Nix vs. Hedden) in 1893, the U.S. Supreme Court decided that it is correct for people to call a tomato a vegetable, even though, scientifically speaking, it is a fruit.

So the next time someone tells you to eat your veggies, ask if they really mean fruits instead.

**SKILL PRACTICE** Read the item. Write your response.

1. Can a vegetable grow on a tree? Explain.

2. Based on what you can infer from the text, how are strawberries and walnuts alike?

3. How does the way that scientists classify fruits differ from the way that most people do?

**STRATEGY PRACTICE** On a separate sheet of paper, draw a Venn diagram to show the similarities and differences between fruits and vegetables mentioned in the passage.

**READ THE PASSAGE** Use clues from the passage and your background knowledge to make inferences.

## Skipping Through History

Throughout the 1900s, almost everyone knew how to jump, or "skip," rope. And it wasn't just kids on playgrounds chanting silly rhymes. Champion boxers like Sugar Ray Leonard and Muhammad Ali jumped rope to build stamina and develop quick footwork.

The activity of rope-jumping for fun and exercise has most likely been around for thousands of years. Historians believe children in ancient Egypt used vines to skip with. A calendar from the 6th century shows Chinese children skipping rope, and medieval European paintings show children skipping rope on cobblestone streets.

The earliest jump ropers in North America may have been Dutch immigrants, who brought the game Double Dutch with them in the 1600s. In Double Dutch, two turners, or "enders," each hold the ends of two long ropes and turn them in opposite directions as one person jumps between them. When the game was first introduced, girls were not encouraged to participate, partly because they were considered weaker, and exercise was thought of as unfeminine. Also, girls wore long dresses that got in the way.

Once girls did start jumping, however, they really took over, and for a while, it was mainly girls who excelled at the activity. Now, both girls and boys jump rope. Jumping rope has become a worldwide competitive sport in which children and adults compete in both singles and team events.

So, pick up a rope, find a silly rhyme or your favorite song, and start jumping.

**SKILL PRACTICE** Read the item. Write your response.

1. How does chanting a rhyme help a person jumping rope?

___

___

2. Why is jumping rope probably popular worldwide?

___

___

3. Quote the line from the text that reveals the author's opinion about jumping rope.

___

___

**STRATEGY PRACTICE** Explain how your background knowledge about jumping rope helped you understand the passage.

___

___

**READ THE PASSAGE** Use clues from the passage to infer information the writer has not directly given.

## The Fleet Sets Sail

It was twilight. Yuen was standing on the deck of a large Chinese junk, gazing at the huge fleet of ships around him—300 ships in all, he had been told. Too many to see in the growing darkness, there were supply ships, battleships, horse transports, and many others. Most ships had 9 masts and 12 sails. Many were more than 450 feet (137 m) long. Since Yuen's junk was near the beginning of the fleet, he had seen Admiral Zheng He sail into the Yellow Sea.

The year was 1403. Thousands of people had lined the Yangzi River to see the armada off that morning. Yuen was only a deckhand, yet he was part of an event unlike anything that had come before it.

Yuen was not yet fully grown. What did he know of the fleet's goals? He knew that this was to be a trading mission. Beyond that? Some said the emperor had directed Zheng He to forge alliances, collect exotic animals, and persuade rulers to pay tribute to China. Others believed the admiral's job was much more than that. They suspected that he had been told to explore civilizations at the ends of the earth, from the most western of the west to the most northern of the north—however far away they might be.

As stars began to appear, Yuen took a bite of pickled fruit. He watched a man take out a strange instrument. The man seemed to be measuring the stars.

**SKILL PRACTICE** Read the item. Write your response.

1. How does Yuen feel about being a part of the fleet? Draw inference from the tone of the text.

___

___

2. What can you infer about Chinese knowledge of the stars in 1403? How do you know?

___

___

3. Describe a *junk*.

___

___

**STRATEGY PRACTICE** Write two facts about ancient China you discovered while reading the passage.

___

___

___

**READ THE PASSAGE** Look for similarities and differences between handcycling and other sports, and use clues from the passage to make inferences about handcycling.

## Handcycling: A Growing Competition Sport

Military veterans Carlos Moleda and Melissa Stockwell aren't the kind of athletes to let any obstacle slow them down. Despite injuries they suffered in combat—Moleda was paralyzed from the waist down and Stockwell lost her left leg—both are now world-class competitors in the growing sport of handcycling.

In the 1980s, designers working on a new type of cycle created one that was powered with the muscles in the arms and upper body, not by feet and legs. Soon after, people with mobility challenges used these handcycles for fun, for exercise, and to participate in competitive races.

Like wheelchair racing, handcycling takes stamina and strong arms. But while wheelchair racers use their arms to push their wheelchairs' rims, handcyclists turn a crank in front of them. The crank works like the foot pedals on a bicycle. Wheelchair racers also tilt forward in their seats. Handcyclists, on the other hand, are often lying or leaning back on their cycle. However, models are also available for those who are more comfortable sitting or kneeling than reclining.

Rory McCarthy manufactures handcycles in Maine. "A lot of our users are veterans," he says. "These men and women who have been badly injured in Iraq and Afghanistan are incredible people. They aren't going to let their injuries or challenges keep them from doing their very best." Considering how skilled and fit the athletes are at handcycle competitions, McCarthy isn't exaggerating.

**SKILL PRACTICE** Read the item. Write your response.

1. Draw two conclusions about Moleda and Stockwell.

_______________________________________________

_______________________________________________

2. How is wheelchair racing similar to handcycling?

_______________________________________________

_______________________________________________

3. How is handcycling different from riding an ordinary bicycle?

_______________________________________________

_______________________________________________

**STRATEGY PRACTICE** How is handcycling like other sports you know of?

_______________________________________________

_______________________________________________

**READ THE PASSAGE** Think about what Louis Armstrong did and the type of person he was.

## Satchmo the Great

Louis Armstrong, nicknamed "Satchmo," was born in 1901 in New Orleans. At that time, jazz music was just becoming popular, and the young Armstrong loved the sound of New Orleans jazz. He started playing the cornet, a brass instrument similar to a trumpet. As a teenager, Armstrong spent many hours listening to local musicians play jazz. He started playing in bands himself and became famous locally.

In 1922, Armstrong moved to Chicago and got a job playing the trumpet in Oliver's Creole Jazz Band. Before long, Armstrong was considered one of the greatest trumpet players of all time. He played with many bands, moving from Chicago to New York and back to Chicago. In 1925, he made his first recordings as the leader of his own group, Louis Armstrong and His Hot Five.

In the 1930s, Armstrong toured the United States and Europe. He began acting in movies, too. He stopped playing the New Orleans jazz of his youth and instead played and sang popular songs with well-known big bands. His swing-style trumpet influenced many later jazz horn players. His throaty yet smooth and rhythmic singing style was also influential. He developed a technique of singing called scat, in which the singer sings jazzy, quick-moving melodies with random nonsense syllables instead of words. Supposedly, he invented scat singing when he dropped his sheet music and could not remember the song's words.

Armstrong died in 1971. Today he is remembered not only as a great trumpeter but also as a bandleader, singer, and film star.

**SKILL PRACTICE** Read the item. Write your response.

1. How did growing up in New Orleans influence Louis Armstrong's life?

_______________________________________________

_______________________________________________

2. What can you tell about Armstrong based on where he played and traveled?

_______________________________________________

_______________________________________________

3. Name two adjectives that describe Armstrong. Explain your choices.

_______________________________________________

_______________________________________________

**STRATEGY PRACTICE** Reread the passage and then list three of Louis Armstrong's important accomplishments.

_______________________________________________

_______________________________________________

**READ THE PASSAGE** Think about the type of people Kano and Saigo were and what 19th-century Japan was like.

## A Heavenly Lord of Judo

The word *judo* means "the way of gentleness" in Japanese. Judo is a Japanese martial art, and its participants use balance, power, and movement—rather than kicking or punching—to overcome their opponents. Judo was created in the 1880s from an earlier martial art called jiujitsu, which is over 500 years old. Jiujitsu was developed as a fighting technique for the warrior class of Japan, but judo focuses more on a code of behavior and a way of living.

Judo was founded by Dr. Jigoro Kano. As a teenager in Japan, Kano was weak and small. He began studying jiujitsu at several schools to improve his strength and confidence. However, Kano thought the jiujitsu schools were unnecessarily violent and rough. So he developed a martial art that was not dangerous to practice and wouldn't needlessly injure people. It was built on the idea that a smaller and weaker person could defeat a stronger opponent by using the opponent's own strength against himself or herself.

One of Kano's first students was Shiro Saigo, born in Japan in 1866. Saigo originally wanted to be an army general but was told he was too short to enter the military. He began studying judo with Kano and trained all day, every day. In 1886, Saigo participated in the Tokyo Metropolitan Police Judo vs. Jiujitsu competition. The competition was arranged to determine which sport was superior. In his final match, Saigo was thrown several times by his much larger opponent, yet always landed gracefully on his feet. Finally, he used a special move to throw his opponent, winning the match and the competition.

As a result of this great victory, Saigo became an idol in Japan. He reached the highest level in judo in 1889. Today, he is considered one of the Four Heavenly Lords, the four best early students of judo.

**SKILL PRACTICE** Read the item. Write your response.

1. What conclusion can you draw about life and males in Japan during the 1880s?

_______________________________________________

_______________________________________________

2. Where and when did the judo versus jiujitsu competition occur?

_______________________________________________

_______________________________________________

3. Name two ways in which judo differs from jiujitsu.

_______________________________________________

**STRATEGY PRACTICE** Describe how you visualized Saigo's judo match.

_______________________________________________

_______________________________________________

**READ THE PASSAGE** Think about how the writer feels about Doctors Without Borders.

## Medicine for Those in Need

Doctors Without Borders is an organization created by doctors and journalists in 1971. It provides medical aid to people in more than 60 countries who are threatened by violence, epidemics, natural disasters, or lack of health care. Doctors Without Borders has more than 27,000 workers helping people around the world on any given day. The workers often see violence and neglect. Although the organization doesn't take sides in political disputes, it may speak out against the conditions that its workers observe and may try to bring attention to a problem.

Nurse Lenny Krommenhoek works with Doctors Without Borders. Recently, she traveled to a remote area of Chad, a country in Africa, to vaccinate children after a measles outbreak. For five weeks she traveled from village to village. Each morning, she rose at 5 AM, dealt with truck breakdowns on terrible roads, and built vaccination sites at each village. There was barely enough water for drinking and none for washing in the communities she visited. She slept on a mattress on the ground, covered with a mosquito net. One great challenge was keeping the vaccines cold in temperatures that rose as high as 104°F (40°C). The vaccines had to be kept at about 40°F (4.4°C). They were transported every few days from a base camp.

At the end of her time in Chad, Krommenhoek reported that despite the hardships, she was glad to have been part of such a "beautiful" assignment.

**SKILL PRACTICE** Read the item. Write your response.

1. What is the theme of this text?

______________________________________________

______________________________________________

2. Describe two personal hardships that Lenny Krommenhoek faced in Chad.

______________________________________________

______________________________________________

3. Based on information in the text, infer the author's opinion of Doctors Without Borders.

______________________________________________

______________________________________________

**STRATEGY PRACTICE** Explain how you stayed focused on the passage as you read.

______________________________________________

______________________________________________

**READ THE FOLK TALE** Look for the lesson or moral in the folk tale.

## The Turtle Who Talked Too Much

In India long ago, there was a proud turtle who talked all the time. One afternoon he heard two hunters discussing their plan to catch turtles the next day, and he became very nervous. He thought and thought about how he could save himself.

Then he found two cranes in a nearby pond. He said, "Beautiful birds, you have such graceful wings. And your white feathers are lovelier than fresh-fallen snow. Perhaps you would be willing to use your powerful wings and feathers to help a friend. Hunters plan to catch me tomorrow. If you will agree to hold a stick between your beaks, I can hold on to it with my teeth. Then you can fly away and carry me to a safe place." The cranes, flattered by the turtle's kind words, agreed to the turtle's plan.

When the hunters came back the next day, the birds took up the stick, and the turtle latched on to it with his mouth. The cranes flapped their wings forcefully, carrying him high into the air, just as the turtle had planned. Some people far below caught sight of the birds flying with the turtle and cried out, "What clever birds they are, to figure out how to carry a turtle!"

When he heard that, the turtle could not help shouting out, "It was my idea!" Of course, as soon as he opened his mouth, he let go of the stick and tumbled to the ground.

**SKILL PRACTICE** Read the item. Write your response.

1. Why is the turtle afraid?

_______________________________________________

_______________________________________________

2. How does the turtle convince the cranes to help him?

_______________________________________________

_______________________________________________

3. What is the moral (theme) of this folk tale?

_______________________________________________

_______________________________________________

**STRATEGY PRACTICE** Write the words or phrases from the passage that were the easiest for you to visualize.

_______________________________________________

_______________________________________________

**READ THE LETTER** Think about the theme of the letter and what it tells you about the kind of person Malia is.

## One House at a Time

Dear Aunt Keema,

I just got back from New Orleans, and it was a life-changing trip. I have blisters on top of my blisters from hammering and sawing!

The neighborhood where we worked was almost completely destroyed. I couldn't believe how much damage a hurricane could cause. Houses were left in piles of rubble, cars were rusted and ruined, and piles of trash flowed from curbs and yards into the street. It is too easy to see how sad it is for the people who live here.

Our class focused on helping to build a house for the DuLac family. We built it on the foundation of their old house, which was the only part that remained. You know, I've never even hammered a nail before, but now I can put on roof shingles and hang a door like a pro! The whole class worked incredibly hard all week, and the DuLacs worked side by side with us. Mr. DuLac taught us some Cajun folk songs, and Ms. DuLac taught us how to use a level and how to hold a hammer properly. They called each of us "Honey" or "Sweetie," just like we were one huge family.

When we finished, the house was beautiful—simple but very sturdy. No hurricane will knock this house over! Even though it was just one house out of the thousands that need rebuilding, I feel like we've done something important. Leaving was both a happy and sad moment for me. The DuLacs were so grateful. It's funny, but I was grateful, too.

Love,
Malia

**SKILL PRACTICE** Read the item. Write your response.

1. What is the theme of this letter?

_______________________________________________

_______________________________________________

2. What did New Orleans look like when Malia arrived?

_______________________________________________

3. How does Malia feel about the work she completed? Quote a line from the text that supports your response.

_______________________________________________

**STRATEGY PRACTICE** Write two sentences from the letter that helped you understand the theme.

_______________________________________________

_______________________________________________

**READ THE PASSAGE** Think about why the author wrote about this topic.

## Soup: A Healthy Choice

If you want to make a great, healthy meal, why not start with a soup? The liquid in soup keeps you feeling full for a long time, and you can add many healthy ingredients—not only to make it delicious but to get your vitamins and minerals. Another great thing about soup is that you can use what you already have in your cupboard or refrigerator to make it.

For example, if you have a quart of chicken or vegetable broth, add it to a pot of water for the base. Throw in a few dried herbs, such as dill or bay leaves, as the pot heats up. If you have a small onion and a clove of garlic, peel and add them, too. Then check the vegetable drawer in your refrigerator. If you find celery or carrots, chop up about a cup of each and toss them in. Green beans, cabbage, and zucchini also work well to add flavor, and you can even use frozen vegetables, such as peas or corn. Next, make your soup extra hearty and high in fiber by adding brown rice or whole-grain pasta. For protein, throw in cooked chicken or canned pinto beans.

Finally, bring the mixture to a boil, and then let it simmer for a while so that the vegetables become tender and the flavors blend together. This usually takes at least 30 minutes. But once it's ready, you'll see that this yummy meal was worth the wait!

**SKILL PRACTICE** Read the item. Write your response.

1. What is the author's purpose for writing this text?

2. Why does the author suggest so many different ingredients?

3. What is the author's purpose for writing the final sentence?

**STRATEGY PRACTICE** Write a question you thought of while reading the passage. If you found the answer, write it, too.

**READ THE PASSAGE** Think about the author's purpose for writing the passage.

## "Aunt" Ida

In 1983, collectors found a remarkably complete fossil in a slate quarry in Messel, Germany. They removed the fossil and in the process separated it into two large pieces. However, it wasn't until scientists began to study the fossil in 2007 that they realized its importance.

Ida, as the fossilized creature is now called, lived about 47 million years ago, and yet its fossil is so well preserved that scientists can tell what the animal ate for its last meal by looking at its digestive tract. What else makes Ida so important? The fossil gives scientists a look at the kind of primates that lived before anthropoids and prosimians developed into two distinct groups. Anthropoids are the animal group that includes humans and apes, while prosimians are the group that includes small monkeys such as lemurs.

From the fossil, scientists can tell that Ida was about the size of a cat. It had features found today in both anthropoids and prosimians. For example, it had opposable thumbs, like humans do. Ida's skeleton looked like a lemur's but did not have the fused teeth that a lemur has on its lower jaw. The creature also lacked the lemur's claws or thin face. Jens Franzen, a scientist working with the fossil, says that although Ida may not be our great-great-grandmother, she is our great-great-great aunt.

**SKILL PRACTICE** Read the item. Write your response.

1. Why does the author include information about how Ida differed from today's lemurs?

______________________________________________

______________________________________________

2. Why does the author mention the kind of thumbs that Ida had?

______________________________________________

______________________________________________

3. Why does the author include Jens Franzen's thoughts at the end of the text?

______________________________________________

______________________________________________

**STRATEGY PRACTICE** What connection did you make with the information in the text? How did it help you better understand the passage?

______________________________________________

______________________________________________

______________________________________________

**READ THE PASSAGE** Use clues from the passage and your background knowledge to make predictions.

## Oona and Finn McCool

Long ago, on an island near Ireland, a giant named Finn McCool lived with his clever wife Oona. Oona and Finn had a good life except for one problem. An unfriendly giant named Cuhullin lived across the river. Finn had never met this giant, but he feared Cuhullin nonetheless.

One day, Cuhullin challenged Finn to a contest of strength. Finn was a strong giant, but he knew that Cuhullin was stronger still, and Finn was worried. Oona, wanting to help her husband, thought of a plan.

On the day that Cuhullin was to arrive, Oona dressed Finn up like a baby and put him into a giant crib. She also decorated an iron frying pan so that it looked like a frosted cake. Finn shook with fear as he waited for his enemy.

When the giant Cuhullin arrived, Oona told him that Finn was not at home. Then she introduced him to the "baby" Finn. Cuhullin was understandably surprised at the size of the child and wondered how large Finn must be to have a baby that size. Oona asked Cuhullin to get her some water. When he started off to the river with a pail, Oona explained, "Oh, Finn usually carries the house to the water." Cuhullin did his best not to look surprised, but he was not very happy at the idea that Finn was so strong.

Finally, Oona offered Cuhullin the cake. She gave him the frosted frying pan, and when he took a bite, he nearly broke a tooth. "This is as hard as a rock!" said Cuhullin.

"Oh, that's the way Finn likes it. Look, even the baby likes it that way," she said, pointing to Finn in the crib. She had given Finn a real cake, and he ate it happily. Cuhullin, suddenly no longer wanting to meet Finn, started making excuses about needing to go home.

**SKILL PRACTICE** Read the item. Write your response.

1. What will Cuhullin do next?

______________________________

______________________________

2. What will Oona do if Cuhullin opts to wait for Finn to get home?

______________________________

______________________________

3. What will Finn do if Cuhullin leaves?

______________________________

**STRATEGY PRACTICE** Write the question you thought of before you read. If you found the answer, write it, too.

______________________________

______________________________

**READ THE PASSAGE** Make predictions about what will happen next.

## Two Friends

One autumn day, two friends, Koji and Kevin, were on their way to school. As they approached their bus stop, Koji saw the bus pull away. "Oh no!" said Koji. "We'll never make it to school before the first bell."

"Oh well," said Kevin, "it's a beautiful day. Let's walk to school. If we run, we might even make it in time."

At lunchtime, both Koji and Kevin realized that they had forgotten to bring their lunches from home. "Oh no!" said Koji. "I'll be starving by the end of the day!"

"Oh well," said Kevin. "I think that if we ask some of our friends, we'll be able to borrow enough money."

After lunch, the two boys had math class together, and Mrs. Miller announced that she was giving them a pop quiz.

"Oh no!" said Koji. "I hate quizzes!"

"We'll do fine," said Kevin. "We didn't have any problems when we worked on our math homework together earlier this week."

Just then, the fire alarm sounded. Although the principal quickly announced through the loudspeakers that it was a fire drill and not a real fire, everyone had to leave their belongings and go outside.

**SKILL PRACTICE** Read the item. Write your response.

1. How will Koji probably react to the fire drill?

2. How do you think Kevin will react to the fire drill?

3. The next school day is photo day, and neither boy remembers to wear his favorite shirt. Predict how each boy will react.

**STRATEGY PRACTICE** How are Koji and Kevin like people you know?

 

**READ THE PASSAGE** Think about why the author wrote the passage, and make predictions about what will likely happen next.

## The Mural Arts Program of Philadelphia

More than twenty-five years ago, Philadelphia started a program to combat graffiti on public buildings. Instead of illegally "tagging" buildings, graffiti artists were given the chance to make murals on building walls in their communities. Now, close to 4,000 murals have been created through the program, which has taken off in neighborhoods across the city.

First known as the Philadelphia Anti-Graffiti Network, the program was renamed the Mural Arts Program in 1996. In 2001, it became part of the city's human services department. Since then, the program has worked with young people who are in detention centers or homeless shelters, or who are in other difficult situations. The program has also helped teach high school students how to make murals and provides after-school and summer arts education activities.

When Charles, Prince of Wales, and his wife, Camilla, the Duchess of York, visited Philadelphia, they took part in an arts activity through the Mural Arts Program. Famous artists such as Kent Twitchell and Sidney Goodman have painted murals for the program. So have at-risk youth and prison inmates. Philadelphia was given the name City of Murals in honor of the program's work. Visitors can tour the murals with a tour guide or take a self-guided tour using a map from the program's website: http://www.muralarts.org.

**SKILL PRACTICE** Read the item. Write your response.

1. What is the author's purpose for writing this text?

_______________________________________________

_______________________________________________

2. Cite text evidence that proves the Mural Arts Program of Philadelphia is famous.

_______________________________________________

_______________________________________________

3. Why does the author include a website at the end of the text?

_______________________________________________

_______________________________________________

**STRATEGY PRACTICE** Write a question about information from the passage. Then ask a partner to answer it.

_______________________________________________

_______________________________________________

**READ THE PASSAGE** Pay attention to the nonfiction text features.

## Having Fun in Ancient Greece

Just as we do today, the ancient Greeks had various ways of amusing themselves. They played games, held sporting events, attended theatrical performances, and listened to music and poetry. Here are some of the forms of entertainment that the Greeks enjoyed.

**Music and Poetry:** Poetry was recited in public places. It was often accompanied by music. Performers called *rhapsodists* (RAP-suh-dists) memorized and performed long poems such as *The Odyssey* by Homer. Although we don't know what Greek music sounded like, we know ancient Greeks used drums, pipes, and stringed instruments.

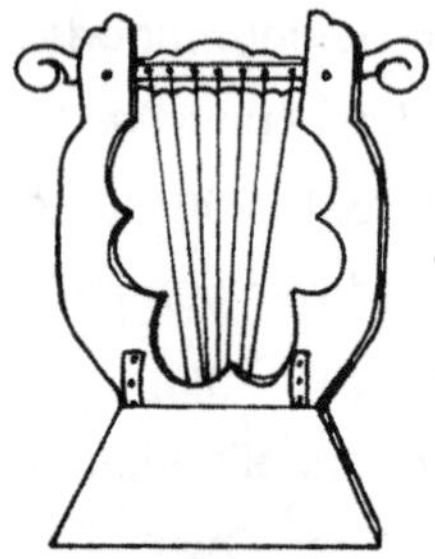

**Toys:** Young children played with games and toys just as young children do today. Yo-yos, clay dolls, and wooden horses with wheels were popular among Greek boys and girls.

**Games:** This painting from an ancient Greek vase shows two warriors playing a board game. The Egyptians played a game called Senet. Might these Greek warriors have been playing Senet, or could it have been chess?

**Theater:** The ancient Greeks loved the theater. Actors dressed in costumes, and many wore masks. Sometimes actors appeared as birds or other animals.

**SKILL PRACTICE** Read the item. Write your response.

1. Why did the author include the information in parentheses?

______________________________

2. What information is included under the subheading "Toys:"?

______________________________

______________________________

3. What does the vase's illustration show? How do you know?

______________________________

______________________________

**STRATEGY PRACTICE** Write one important fact or idea that you learned from the passage.

______________________________

______________________________

**READ THE PASSAGE** Pay attention to how the writer has organized the information.

## Newton's Laws of Motion

Have you ever heard of Newton's Laws of Motion? These three laws, or principles, explain how things move.

**Law 1:** An object at rest stays at rest. A moving object keeps moving. Objects continue doing what they're doing unless a stronger force acts on them.

*Here, the stronger force is the wall. It stops the truck but not the boxes, so they keep moving backward.*

**Law 2:** It takes more force to move a heavy object than to move a lighter object. Newton came up with a scientific formula to explain this:

**F**orce = **M**ass x **A**cceleration

*Large weights with a lot of mass require more force to lift than smaller, lighter weights do.*

**Law 3:** For every force, there is an equal reaction in the opposite direction.

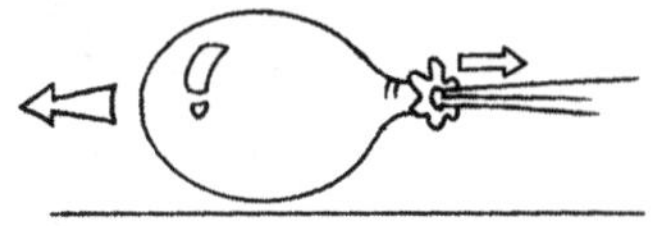

*Air from an untied balloon rushes out in one direction. As the air escapes, it pushes the balloon in the opposite direction.*

**SKILL PRACTICE** Read the item. Write your response.

1. How do the captions help the reader to understand the drawings?

2. How do the illustrations help the reader to understand the Laws of Motion?

3. *It takes less force to move a light object than to move a heavier object.* Use text evidence to prove this statement true or false.

**STRATEGY PRACTICE** Explain how the columns used to organize the text helped you understand the information.

**READ THE PASSAGE** Read the passage and study the diagram to learn about ships called brigantines.

# The Brigantine

**People have always been fascinated by pirates. The sailing ships on which pirates traveled the seas long ago were magnificent boats. This diagram shows one common type of ship they used, called the brigantine, or brig. Many pirates in the 1700s preferred the brig because it was light and fast. It also had a large cargo hold for plenty of pirates' loot!**

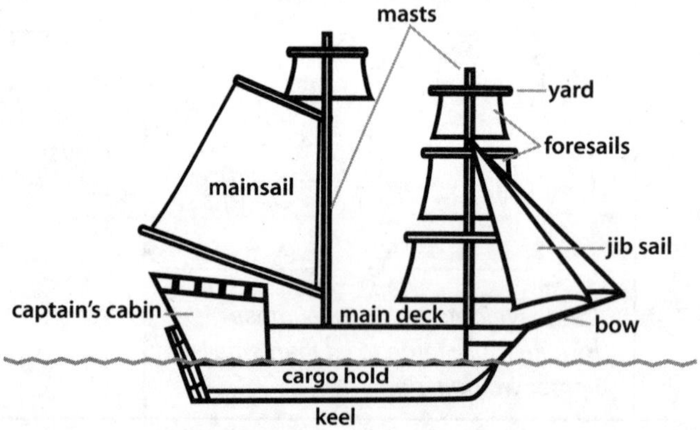


*A brig is a "square-rigged" sailing ship, which means that the primary sails are at right angles to the length of the ship. They hang from strong horizontal poles called yards, which are at right angles to the mast.*

**SKILL PRACTICE** Read the item. Write your response.

1. How many yards are shown in the diagram?

2. On the ship, what is on the opposite end from the bow?

3. What is the area below the main deck called?

**STRATEGY PRACTICE** How would you describe a brigantine to someone who had never seen or heard of one before?

**READ THE PASSAGE** Read slowly and pause after each paragraph.

## Mesoamerica Before the Spanish

Long before the Spanish invaded Central America, a number of civilizations existed in the area now known as Mesoamerica. The map and timeline below provide dates and locations of a few of these extraordinary cultures.

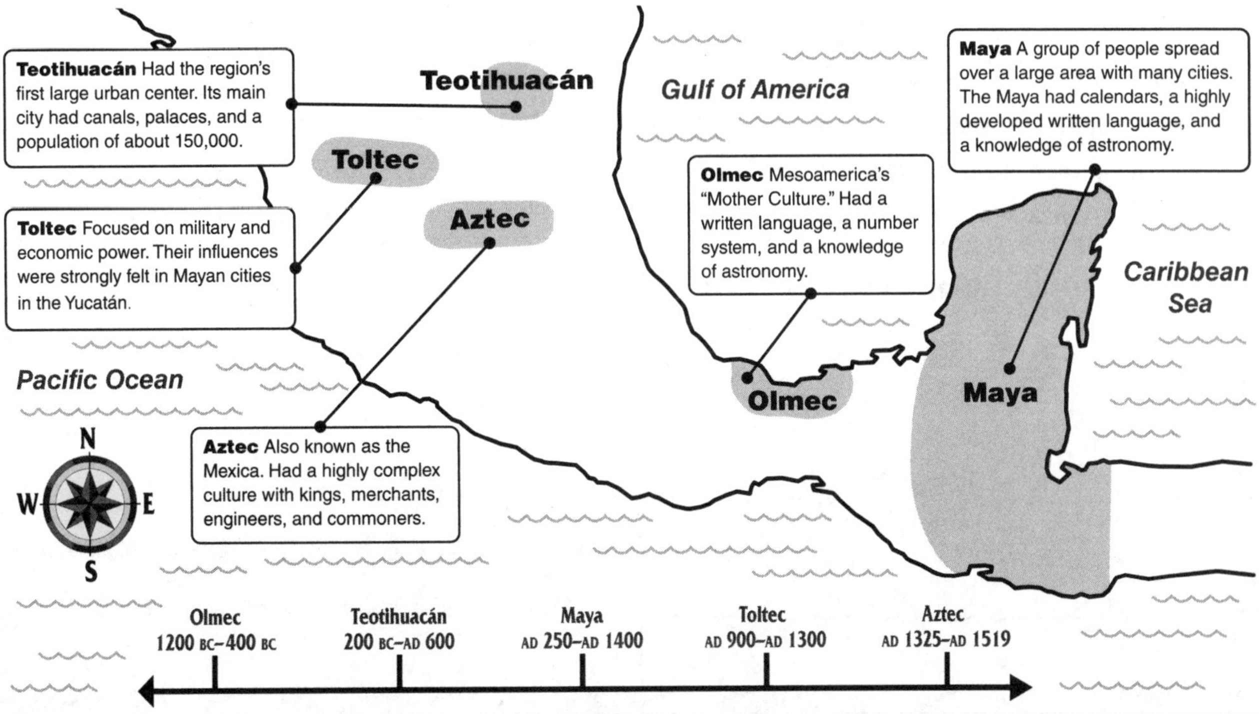


**SKILL PRACTICE** Read the item. Write your response.

1. What is the purpose of the map?

2. Use the timeline to determine which culture's existence did *not* occur simultaneously with the Maya.

3. Which culture was located the farthest north? How can you tell?

**STRATEGY PRACTICE** How are the map and timeline connected?

**READ THE BROCHURE** Look carefully at the text features and visual information.

# The Experience of a Lifetime!

Swim with the dolphins in our private saltwater lagoon at Punta Roo, Mexico.

- Experienced and knowledgeable trainers
- Relaxed, up-close interaction with dolphins
- Sessions every half-hour from 8:30 a.m. to 5:30 p.m. year-round
- Free transportation from your hotel to Punta Roo

| Session | Duration | Price |
|---|---|---|
| Dolphin Swim | ½ hour | $115** |
| Extended Dolphin Swim | 1 hour | $169** |

Lockers, towels, goggles, and bilingual trainers are included. Photos/DVDs are extra.

**www.dolphinadventurepuntaroo.com**

**Make your reservation online and get a 10% discount.

**SKILL PRACTICE** Read the item. Write your response.

1. What is the primary purpose of this brochure?

______________________________________________

______________________________________________

2. Are DVDs and photos of the dolphin experience included in the price? How do you know?

______________________________________________

______________________________________________

3. Why did the prices end with asterisks?

______________________________________________

**STRATEGY PRACTICE** What is something from the brochure that parents would want to know?

______________________________________________

______________________________________________

# How to Be a Good Reader

Ask yourself these questions to help you understand what you read:

| | |
|---|---|
| **Main Idea and Details** | What is the story mostly about?<br>What tells me more about the main idea? |
| **Sequence** | What happens first, next, and last?<br>What are the steps to do something? |
| **Cause and Effect** | What happens? (the effect)<br>Why did it happen? (the cause) |
| **Evaluate Evidence** | What claims is the author making?<br>What evidence supports these claims? |
| **Compare and Contrast** | How are these people or things the same?<br>How are these people or things different? |
| **Make Inferences** | What clues does the story give?<br>What do I know already that will help? |
| **Prediction** | What clues does the story give?<br>What do I know already that will help?<br>What will happen next? |
| **Character and Setting** | Who or what is the story about?<br>Where and when does the story take place? |
| **Theme** | What lesson does this story teach?<br>How does the author feel about this topic? |
| **Author's Purpose** | Does the story entertain, inform, try to persuade me, or teach me how to do something? |
| **Nonfiction Text Features** | What kind of text am I reading?<br>What does it tell me? |
| **Visual Information** | Is there a picture, chart, or graph?<br>What does it tell me? |

# Congratulations!

You have successfully completed

**Daily Reading Comprehension**

# My Notes

# My Notes

# My Notes

# My Notes

# My Notes

# My Notes